10.00

ID0820521

METAPHOR

METAPHOR
A Psychoanalytic View

ROBERT ROGERS

UNIVERSITY OF CALIFORNIA PRESS
Berkeley Los Angeles London

University of California Press
Berkeley and Los Angeles, California
University of California Press, Ltd.
London, England
Copyright © 1978 by
The Regents of the University of California
ISBN 0-520-03548-8
Library of Congress Catalog Card Number: 77-80477
Printed in the United States of America

1 2 3 4 5 6 7 8 9

for Crane
*"who wed himself to things
of light from infancy"*

and Kris
*"whose virtues plead like angels,
trumpet-tongued"*

Contents

Acknowledgments

I wish to thank the editors of *Hartford Studies in Literature* for permission to reprint portions of the material in Chapters 1 and 4 from the following articles: "The Dynamics of Metaphor," *HSL* III (1971): 157-90, and "A Gathering of Roses," *HSL* V (1973): 61-76. An earlier version of Chapter 2 appeared in *The International Journal of Psycho-Analysis* 54 (1973): 61-74 under the title of "On the Metapsychology of Poetic Language: Modal Ambiguity."

This project was funded at various stages by the University Awards Committee of The Research Foundation of the State University of New York in the form of three Faculty Research Fellowships.

From many people I have received personal assistance that has contributed in various ways to the making of this book. I want to acknowledge the stimulation derived from discussing these ideas with my students, especially Susan Foster. John Franzosa and Gail Mortimer provided me with able research assistance. My colleague, Robert Edwards, helped me to gather medieval roses. I am much obliged to Mrs. Joan Cipperman for typing the manuscript. I should like to thank William McClung and Doris Kretschmer of the University of California Press, where the editorial responsibilities were handled with care and enthusiasm. I am indebted to Mr. McClung for what, in retrospect, seems like extraordinary patience and trust.

Most of whatever clinical awareness I have managed to acquire during the past few years I owe to the guidance of Lloyd Clarke, Antony Foti, Fleming James III, Dorothy Adema, and Murray Morphy; to the members of the Case Presentation Seminar at the University Health Service; and to my fellow participants in that exhilarating experiment held—and still going on—at the training ground know locally as 67S.

Advice that I sought was freely given by three people from the department of psychology at SUNY-Buffalo: Joseph Masling, Edward Katkin, and the late Marvin Feldman.

Earlier versions of portions of this book and related material were presented as work-in-progress to the Buffalo Group for Applied Psychoanalysis. I cannot overstate the value of these opportunities, nor can I separate the catalytic virtue of this group from that of being associated for several years with members of the Center for the Psychological Study of the Arts. Among these many associates I have learned from, I would like to single out three: Heinz Lichtenstein, for the example he has provided, and Murray Schwartz and Norman Holland for the intellectual leadership they have exercised through their "presence at the center."

In addition to drawing on their published work, I am beholden to Mark Kanzer, Charles Rycroft, and Roy Schafer for communicating with me about some of the knottier theoretical issues at stake in trying to speak of language in terms of metapsychology. Roy Schafer's recent book, *A New Language for Psychoanalysis,* almost persuaded me to abandon metapsychology altogether. If I was finally unwilling to do so, it is no fault of his!

For their professional concern I am grateful to my former teacher, Frederick Wyatt, to my beloved editor, Leonard Manheim, and to my colleague, Mark Shechner, who was ready and unstinting in his support of my work at a time when I very much needed it.

My greatest debts are to the tough-minded friends who read and criticized this book in its original version: Herbert Schneidau and David Willbern.

Finally, I want to thank my wife Joanne for her proofreading, her understanding, and for putting up with all my transfers.

Quantum theory thus provides us with a striking illustration of the fact that we can fully understand a connection though we can only speak of it in images and parables. In this case, the images and parables are by and large the classical concepts, i.e., "wave" and "corpuscle." They do not fully describe the real world and are, moreover, complementary in part, and hence contradictory. For all that, since we can only describe natural phenomena with our everyday language, we can only hope to grasp the real facts by means of these images.

—attributed to Niels Bohr by Werner Heisenberg

Perhaps the reason why so many metaphors have a peculiarly poignant beauty is because each of them kindles in us momentarily a dim memory of the time when we lost the outer world—when we first realized that the outer world *is* outside, and we are unbridgeably apart from it, and alone. Further, the *mutual sharing* of such metaphorical experience would seem, thus, to be about as intimate a psychological contact as adult human beings can have with one another.

—Harold Searles, *Collected Papers on Schizophrenia*

PROLOGUE

Cloven Tongues
Like as of Fire

What is more potent than fire?
—Hawthorne, "The Devil in Manuscript"

As part of his explanation in *The Scarlet Letter* of Dimmesdale's extraordinary power to stir the hearts of his congregation, Hawthorne alludes to the linguistic miracle portrayed in the second chapter of Acts, the moment when the apostles are inspired by a visitation of the Holy Ghost to speak in tongues: "And suddenly there came a sound from heaven as of a rushing mighty wind, and it filled all the house where they were sitting. And there appeared unto them cloven tongues like as of fire, and it sat upon each of them. And they were all filled with the Holy Ghost, and began to speak with other tongues, as the Spirit gave them utterance." All men who listen can understand the apostles' words, no matter what their native language.

Hawthorne expands on the relevance of his biblical allusion to the action of the novel. Dimmesdale's older colleagues cannot reach their audiences effectively. Though some are scholars, steeped in the abstruse lore of divinity, and some are men with a greater share of "shrewd, hard, iron or granite understanding," and some are even "true saintly fathers," of patient thought

1

"etherialized . . . by spiritual communications with the better world," Dimmesdale's ability leaves his fellow ministers of the gospel far behind. What these men lack and what Dimmesdale possesses, we are told, is "the gift that descended upon the chosen disciples, at Pentecost, in tongues of flame; symbolizing, it would seem, not the power of speech in foreign and unknown languages, but that of addressing the whole human brotherhood in the heart's native language." These fathers, "otherwise so apostolic, lacked Heaven's last and rarest attestation of their office, the Tongue of Flame. They would have vainly sought—had they ever dreamed of seeking—to express the highest truths through the humblest medium of familiar words and images." Hawthorne emphasizes Dimmesdale's "power of experiencing and communicating emotion" and stresses the connection between the minister's passionate eloquence and his secret burden of guilt: "This very burden it was, that gave him sympathies so intimate with the sinful brotherhood of mankind; so that his heart vibrated in unison with theirs, and received their pain into itself, and sent its own throb of pain through a thousand other hearts, in gushes of sad, persuasive eloquence." Dimmesdale's parishioners fancy him a mouthpiece of heaven. They regard the ground he walks on as sanctified. Virgins grow pale around him, "victims of a passion so imbued with religious sentiment that they imagined it to be all religion, and brought it openly, in their white bosoms, as their most acceptable sacrifice before the altar."

Oddly enough, Hawthorne never makes us privy to any of Dimmesdale's stirring sermons. He does not need to in order to have us accept the illusion he creates of Dimmesdale's gift because we already know, intuitively, that Hawthorne himself possesses the Tongue of Flame. Hawthorne addresses the whole human brotherhood in the heart's native language. He conveys truths through the humblest medium of familiar words and images. He stirs guilt and passion in his readers.

Hawthorne's rendering of the Pentecostal miracle seems to me to be paradigmatic of the nature of artistic communication, especially verbal communication, so I will use it as a lens for bringing into focus the subject of this book: psychological aspects of the metaphoric process. When brought to bear, this lens makes certain aspects of Hawthorne's treatment of Dimmesdale's eloquence assume heuristic value.

To begin with, there is something mysterious, almost magical, in the minister's art. "The people knew not the power that moved them thus." When Hawthorne mentions Dimmesdale's "power of experiencing and communicating emotion," he indicates that the minister's magic has more to do with emotions than with ideas. These emotions appear to be conveyed indirectly rather than directly and to be received more unconsciously than consciously. What occurs, in fact, is not so much communication as a special form of communion, a sharing: Dimmesdale's heart "vibrated in unison with theirs, and received their pain into itself, and sent its own throb of pain through a thousand other hearts." This kind of magical ability to transmit turbulent messages through unconscious channels accords well with a wide array of modern assumptions about the psychology of artistic communication. Communication of this kind can only involve the old, not the new, the known, not the unknown, the universal, not the arcane. It must be based on a measure of shared life experience or else no significant communication of the kind Dimmesdale specializes in can take place. Psychoanalysis locates this shared life experience in man's epigenetic development. Such an assumption would in this case help to explain why none of the parishioners *understand* Dimmesdale's secret guilt—or believe in it—though all of them can *feel* it and *share* it. They share what in Christian terms was called original sin but what in psychological terms has more to do with the inevitable anxiety and conflict connected with our origin and growth as human beings. While it does not lie within my purpose to try to trace such origins with respect to this novel, I might suggest, in passing, that a hint of the oedipal origins of Dimmesdale's crime appears in the erotic triangle of the novel and that a sexual component of the tongue of flame emerges in the unconscious lovesick passion the minister's words imbue in the young virgins of his congregation, though they mistake their emotions for purely spiritual ones.

A number of other implications for the study of language processes lie compacted in the primal metaphor Hawthorne invokes from the Bible. The very ambiguity of the tongue of flame suggests that ambiguity itself suffuses poetic language. Since tongues of flame must be in motion, the metaphor belongs to the class Aristotle calls "active" to distinguish them from the less effective static variety. By extension, poetic imagery is something dynamic. It is part of a process and not simply material which has been processed. This metaphoric process often involves a creative redundancy. Flames are tongue-like and tongues may be flame-like. The latter transfer seems more poetic. To speak of a tongue of flame while watching a hearthfire amounts to using a dead metaphor, whereas to speak of a tongue of flame in the context of power, passion, inspiration, generation, and communication amounts to poetry. Despite its twofoldedness, the tongue of flame metaphor is not "mixed" because the two separate images, metaphors themselves, fuse into a complex metaphor in precisely that "esemplastic" manner Coleridge associates with the act of imagination. Throughout this book I will be concerned with these matters: with the dynamic processes involved in creating and responding to metaphor, with the ambiguity underlying these dynamics, and with correlations between imagery and imagination.

In the very commonness of its component images the tongue of flame metaphor illustrates as well as any what Hawthorne means when he praises Dimmesdale for relying on "the humblest medium of *familiar* words and images." The value of Hawthorne's point may be difficult to appreciate because people tend to take the commonplace for granted. Noam Chomsky talks about this problem in *Language and Mind.* He says that in matters pertaining to language and psychology the very familiarity of the phenomena constitutes a hindrance because of the intellectual effort needed to see that such phenomena pose problems serious enough to call for intricate theoretical explanations.[1] Perhaps the true importance and potential complexity of simple language can be illustrated by considering—first in isolation and then in context—a series of words constituting the main images of a memorable passage of poetry: the body images of hands, eyes, and blood; the activities of plucking, and washing; the ocean; and the colors green and red. These images may seem ordinary to the point of dullness out of context but no one could think so knowing them to be Shakespeare's, spoken when Macbeth hears a knocking shortly after he kills King Duncan:

1. Noam Chomsky, *Language and Mind,* enl. ed. (New York: Harcourt, Brace, Janovich, 1972), p. 24.

What *hands* [the knocking] are here? Ha! They *pluck* out mine *eyes!*
Will all great Neptune's *ocean wash* this *blood*
Clean from my *hand?* No, this my *hand* will rather
The multitudinous *seas* incarnadine,
Making the *green* one *red.*

The words "multitudinous" and "incarnadine" constitute egregious departures from the otherwise simple, native, and predominantly monosyllabic locution of the passage. Shakespeare rarely employs such ornate diction in his mature work, and even in this instance he adds the saving concreteness of "Making the green one red." Without that line the passage would read more like rant than poetry.

I would make one further observation about the phrasing of Hawthorne's claim that Dimmesdale can express "the highest truths through the humblest medium of familiar *words* and *images*." Hawthorne's meaning, or at any rate the meaning I wish to be derived here, becomes clearer by deleting the word "words." One can then say that the most expressive artists will rely not just on language-in-general but rather on the infinite resources of imagery, or metaphor. If possession of the tongue of flame may be said to necessitate employing the humblest medium of familiar images, then the tongue of flame becomes a meta-metaphor. The tongue of flame is a metaphor and Metaphor is the Tongue of Flame. It is primarily in the potentialities of the metaphoric process that the linguistic power of Hawthorne and other literary artists lies. Metaphor may not be the only source but it can only be a major source of their power.

Similar claims for the role of metaphor have often been made by others.[2] Aristotle singles out command of metaphor as the most important element in style and the hallmark of genius. In his

2. Aristotle, *On Poetry and Style,* trans. and ed. G. M.A. Grube (Indianapolis: Liberal Arts Press, 1958), p. 49. Percy Bysshe Shelley, "A Defense of Poetry," in *The Norton Anthology of English Literature,* ed. M. H. Abrams et al. (New York: Norton, 1962), p. 1351. Ortega y Gasset, *The Dehumanization of Art* (Princeton: Princeton University Press, 1968), p. 33. C. Day Lewis, *The Poetic Image* (London: Jonathan Cape, 1947), p. 17. Gaston Bachelard, *The Psychoanalysis of Fire,* trans. Alan C. M. Ross (Boston: Beacon Press, 1964), p. 109. Ernest Fenellosa, "The Chinese Written Character as a Medium for Poetry," in *Prose Keys to Modern Poetry,* ed. Karl Shapiro (New York: Harper & Row, 1962), p. 148. Jacques Derrida, "White Mythology: Metaphor in the Text of Philosophy," *New*

Defense of Poetry Shelley says the language of the poet is "vitally metaphorical." For Ortega y Gasset, metaphor "is perhaps one of man's most fruitful potentialities. Its efficacy verges on magic, and it seems a tool for creation which God forgot inside one of His creatures when He made him." For C. Day Lewis, metaphor remains "the life-principle of poetry, the poet's chief text and glory." For Gaston Bachelard, "a poetic mind is purely and simply a syntax of metaphors." Ernest Fenellosa calls metaphor "the revealer of nature . . . the very substance of poetry." Jacques Derrida sees metaphor in the text of philosophical discourse as a white mythology, or bleached poetry, a trace of a trace of poetry on the slate of abstraction "which yet remains, active and stirring, inscribed in white ink, an invisible drawing covered over in the palimpsest." For Norman O. Brown there isn't anything *but* metaphor. "Everything is only a metaphor; there is only poetry," he declares in his best prophetic manner at the end of *Love's Body.*

Aristotle isolates certain properties of metaphor for special consideration. "Metaphors are a kind of riddle" (*Rhetoric,* 1405 b), he says, thereby making a transfer, or comparison, *in* metaphor *about* metaphor [Gr. *metapherein*: to transfer]. His statement about the nature of metaphor involves a riddle metaphor. His apparent meaning is that metaphors pose implicit questions in much the same way riddles formulate explicit questions about an asserted relationship between two different categories of things. A typical riddle asks, "How is an *x* like a *y?*" whereas a typical metaphor reads, "An *x* is a *y,*" a form of statement begging the question of how *x* resembles *y.* Though good metaphors should be puzzling the way riddles are, continues Aristotle, they ought not to be "farfetched." At the same time he says that good metaphors should be both "lucid" and "strange," the latter word being defined in the *Poetics* (1457 b) as "used by other people," that is, by strangers. Even if "strange" here means something like "fresh", "original," "unhackneyed," a really origi-

---

Literary History VI (Autumn, 1974): 5-74; quotation p. 11. Norman O. Brown, *Love's Body* (New York: Random House, 1966), p. 266.

For a useful bibliographical guide, see Warren A. Shibles, *Metaphor: An Annotated Bibliography and History* (Whitewater, Wisc.: The Language Press, 1971), a work that contains over four hundred pages of listings.

nal metaphor is unlikely to be lucid, at least not at first, and it is even harder to think of metaphors as being at once lucid and puzzling. An answer to the riddle of Aristotle's seeming inconsistency may be the paradox that metaphors can be at once clear and confusing, at once familiar (not farfetched) and mysterious, as in Hamlet's odd figure for the fate of all flesh when he says, "To what base uses we may return, Horatio! Why may not imagination trace the noble dust of Alexander till a' find it stopping a bunghole?" In any case, Aristotle's comparison of metaphors with riddles, besides suggesting that every original metaphor contains a submerged riddle, confronts us with the related possibility that there is something inherently puzzling about metaphor as a class or genus.

One puzzling aspect of the expressive capaciousness of metaphor takes the form of an image's potential for focusing both thought and emotion in a particularly intense, economical way. While concern for intense moments in poetry goes back at least as far as Longinus, who feels that sublime bursts of passion require "exact bold metaphors" for their expression, it is not until the generation of readers we call the New Critics that people return to the issue of intensity frequently enough to warrant my dwelling for a moment on their ideas, some of which have been formative in my own thinking. Reflections on the nature of poetic intensity can be found in Ezra Pound's definition of an image as "an intellectual and emotional complex in an instant of time"; in the attention such cognitively oriented critics as Wimsatt and Beardsley give to the emotional concomitants of poetry in their famous essay on the Affective Fallacy; and in I. A. Richard's insistence that the two main functions of language are the referential and the emotive.[3] A locus classicus of the problem occurs in the very first words of William Empson's brilliant yet disappointing book, *The Structure of Complex Words*: "Emotions, as is well known, are frequently expressed by language; this does not seem one of the ultimate mysteries; but it is extremely

3. Ezra Pound, in Herbert N. Schneidau, *Ezra Pound: The Image and the Real* (Baton Rouge: Louisiana State University Press, 1969), p. 21; W. K. Wimsatt, Jr. and Monroe C. Beardsley, "The Affective Fallacy," in *The Verbal Icon*, ed. W. K. Wimsatt (New York: Farrar, Straus & Giroux, n.d.), pp. 21-39; I. A. Richards, *Principles of Literary Criticism*, 2nd. ed. (London: Routledge & Kegan Paul, Ltd., 1926), pp. 261 ff.

hard to get a consistent and usable theory about their mode of
action. What an Emotive use of language may be, where it crops
up, and whether it should be praised there, is not so much one
question as a protean confusion, harmful in a variety of fields and
particularly rampant in literary criticism."

One way modern formalist criticism locates emotional intensity in poetry is to speak of it somewhat redundantly in terms of
verbal tension and verbal energy, such as when Charles Olson
talks about "the *kinetics* of the thing. A poem is energy transferred from where the poet got it (he will have some several
causations), by way of the poem itself to, all the way over to, the
reader. Okay. Then the poem itself must, at all points, be a high
energy-construct and, at all points, an energy-discharge."[4] Having rejected the static conception of metaphor as ornament derived from the Renaissance idea of style as a garment, modern
writers almost always speak of metaphoric intensity in dynamic
terms of some kind. For Pound, "The image is more than an idea.
It is a vortex or cluster of fused ideas and is endowed with
energy."[5] The meta-metaphor "vortex" illustrates the trend.
Pound remains contemptuous of explanatory, ornamental, and
analogical metaphors. Analogy, he says with superb condescen-
sion, is either "range-finding or fumble." He decries the "di-
luters" of early imagist aesthetics for thinking only of the "sta-
tionary" image, contending that "if you can't think of imagism or
phanopoeia as including the moving image, you will have to
make a really needless division of fixed image and praxis or
action." Pound wants a vital and dynamic poetry—ideally a *pre-
sentational* rather than a *representational* one.

Max Eastman contributes a neurological version of the notion
of verbal tension when he says that art "must arouse a reaction
and yet impede it, creating a tension in our nervous systems
sufficient and rightly calculated to make us completely aware that
we are living something—no matter what." I. A. Richards mocks
this view by saying, "Tie a man down and approach him with a
red-hot poker; you will arouse a reaction and sufficiently impede

4. Charles Olson, untitled statement on his poetics, in *The New American
Poetry: 1945-60,* ed. Donald M. Allen (New York: Grove Press, Inc., 1960), p.
387.

5. Ezra Pound, in Schneidau, *Ezra Pound,* pp. 34, 65.

it to make him completely aware, I believe, that he is living something." Richards himself deals with the idea of verbal tension by articulating a theory of "disparity action" in metaphor, the idea being that the disparities between what he calls "tenor" and "vehicle" are as much if not more productive of poetic energy as are the similarities. Yet Richards ends up in the neurological impasse he teases Max Eastman about when he disclaims the possibility of further understanding the dynamics of metaphor by saying, "We do not yet know enough about the central nervous system."[6]

Without tracing efferent patterns in the neural networks of the central nervous system, and certainly without recourse to the aid of red-hot pokers, I trust it will be possible to demonstrate a psychologically more sophisticated theory of disparity-action in metaphor than was possible for New Critics working without a psychology paying heed to unconscious phenomena. At least I intend to try by employing psychoanalysis.

Until recently, psychoanalytic criticism has tended to focus on the fantasy content of literature rather than on the formal resources language has at its disposal for presenting such material in all its artistic plenitude. For critics like Ernest Jones and K. R. Eissler, the play's the thing when they write about *Hamlet,* not the poem—not the wordplay within the play. As for specific discussions of the nature of metaphor, psychoanalytic commentators have not had much to say beyond a smattering of papers more clinical than theoretical in orientation except for a handful of people like Norman O. Brown and Theodore Thass-Thienemann.[7] I will try to remedy this situation by formulating a model for the dynamics of response to significant metaphor. In addition

6. Max Eastman, *The Literary Mind* (New York: Scribner's, 1932), p. 205; I. A. Richards, *The Philosophy of Rhetoric* (New York: Oxford University Press, 1965), pp. 124-32; and *Principles of Literary Criticism,* p. 251.

7. For a couple of exceptions, see the recent linguistics-oriented psychoanalytic paper by Benjamin B. Rubinstein, "On Metaphor and Related Phenomena," in *Psychoanalysis and Contemporary Science,* Vol. I, ed. Robert R. Holt and Emanuel Peterfreund (New York: International Universities Press), and the papers— also linguistics-oriented—of Victor H. Rosen: "Sign Phenomena and their Relation to Unconscious Meaning," *Int. J. Psycho-Anal.* 50 (1969): 197-207, and "Introduction to Panel on Language and Psychoanalysis," *Ibid.* 50 (1969): 113-16. I will mention other exceptions further on.

I will address the relationship of metaphor to sexuality, to creativity, and to what psychoanalysis so awkwardly calls "object relations," a phrase referring to the structuring of all deep, past-oriented, internalized emotional relationships. I also speak of certain forms of transitional phenomena with respect to metaphor, including presumed relations between writer and reader, and reader and text, as well as transitional phenomena in the sense articulated by D. W. Winnicott.

In an essay published several decades ago John Middleton Murry remarks that discussions of metaphor often seem superficial at first. "Not until we have ourselves made the attempt to get farther do we begin to realize that the investigation of metaphor is curiously like the investigation of any of the primary data of consciousness."[8] At this point Murry goes on to claim that such investigation "cannot be pursued very far without our being led to the borderline of sanity. Metaphor is as ultimate as speech itself, and speech as ultimate as thought. If we try to penetrate them beyond a certain point, we find ourselves questioning the very faculty and instrument with which we are trying to penetrate them. The earth trembles and yawns beneath the explorer's feet." Yes, there were times when I might say that I felt a few tremors—some disequilibrium, at least, and symptoms of disorientation. There were even times when I was sufficiently bewitched by figures of speech to understand what Bachelard means when he says he personally welcomes the poet's image "as a little piece of experimental folly, like a virtual grain of hashish without which it is impossible to enter into the reign of the imagination."[9] This book remains a sober one, however, and tales of wild impetuosities and strange entanglements into which my investigations sometimes led me will have to be told somewhere else, some other time.

Middleton Murry also says in the essay just referred to that to attempt a fundamental examination of metaphor "would be nothing less than an investigation of the genesis of thought itself."

8. John Middleton Murry, "Metaphor," in *Countries of the Mind* (London: Oxford University Press, 1931), p. 1.

9. Gaston Bachelard, *The Poetics of Space*, trans. Maria Jolas (New York: Orion Press, 1964), p. 219.

The development of psychoanalytic theory has made that kind of exploration possible, and I talk about elemental types of mental functioning in the next chapter. It is here that I formulate a theoretical model of the dynamics of response to metaphor based on the assumption that many images in poetry derive their great power from effecting "transfers" of conscious and unconscious "material" in the "mind" of the reader—or in his "heart" or "bowels" or wherever such transactions may be supposed to take place if we ignore what Alfred North Whitehead calls the fallacy of simple location. Corresponding to the problem of *locating* the response of the reader, incidentally, is that of localizing information in a text, a difficulty that has bedeviled information theory for many years.[10] Therefore I cannot emphasize too strongly that while the kind of information communicated by metaphor will for convenience be treated as though it can be localized in a given image on a given page, much discussion later in the book will be designed to show that a great deal of this information is actually dispersed throughout the larger verbal context of the specific metaphoric text, not to mention the relevant information encoded and on tap, as it were, in the mind, heart, bowels, glands, and other organs of the engaged and introjecting reader.

10. See Gregory Bateson, *Steps to an Ecology of Mind* (New York: Ballantine Books, 1972), p. 408.

1

Modes of Mentation

> In the eighteenth century Vico spoke of the meta-
> phorical, imagistic language of the early stages of
> culture; it was left to Freud to discover how, in a
> scientific age, we still feel and think in figurative
> formations, and to create, what psychoanalysis is, a
> science of tropes, of metaphor and its variants, syn-
> ecdoche and metonymy.
> —Lionel Trilling, *The Liberal Imagination*

Henry James discusses "The Jolly Corner" in terms of its being, for him, an adventure story more exciting than one concerning detectives or pirates "or other splendid desperadoes," and he says that when he portrays a character most deeply engaged with the forces of violence, it is then that, "as with the longest and firmest prongs of consciousness, I grasp and hold the throbbing subject." James might have said, "My interest strengthens my grasp of the subject." Instead he offers us a strange but vital figure suggesting, among other things, a terrified victim in the grip of some fierce, predatory animal. Theme as prey? Imagination as predator? At issue is not the meaning of James's curious tropes but the simple fact that even when performing as a literary critic he cannot dispense with his habit, as an artist, of speaking in figures. T. S. Eliot once observed that Henry James had a mind so fine no idea could violate it. This tribute imputes a purity to artistic thought

which is not receptive to ideas in the raw. Artists do not think
with ideas, then, or through them, but with something else or in
some other way. Middleton Murry says flatly, "Novelists and
poets, *qua* novelists and poets, do not really have ideas at all, they
have perceptions, intuitions, emotional convictions."[1]

John Livingston Lowes's *The Road to Xanadu* provides a
similar view of the imaginative processes of the poet. He con-
tends that when Coleridge's imagination was operating in a state
of high tension "actual pictures seem to have passed before it
with the preternatural vividness of those after-images which the
eighteenth century loved to call 'ocular spectra.' " Later he quotes
a passage from the notebooks in which Coleridge mentions "the
streamy nature of association, which thinking curbs and rudders."[2] Here Coleridge calls attention to not one but two different types of mental activity, one of which ("thinking") per-
forms the adjunctive tasks of asserting control and giving direction to the other type. Instead of assuming with Murry that
artistic thought does not involve reason, it might be better to go
along with Coleridge in supposing it to be dual in nature, combining a "streamy," associative, pictorial kind of thought with a
more rigorous and rational type. Such a dualistic view accords
well with the famous passage in *A Midsummer Night's Dream*
where Shakespeare portrays lovers, lunatics, and poets as being "of
imagination all compact," in having "seething brains" and "shaping fantasies" which apprehend "more than cool reason ever
comprehends." This passage does not rule out "cool reason" but
subordinates it to the passionately concrete reach of the imagination.

For heuristic purposes poetic "thought" may be divided into
two categories. One may be characterized as concrete, pictorial,
perceptual, emotional, intuitional, and more imaginative, the
other as abstract, conceptual, less emotional, analytical, more controlled, and less spontaneous. It follows that language embodying
these two types of mental activity will have corresponding attributes. A complete description of these two types would require

1. John Middleton Murry, *The Problem of Style* (London: Oxford University
Press), p. 5.
2. John Livingston Lowes, *The Road to Xanadu* (New York: Houghton
Mifflin, 1927), pp. 66, 72.

the addition of still other attributes, which might result in complicating the two main categories to the point where they would
be almost impossible to identify.[3] How can these two categories
be labelled in such a manner as to synthesize their complex
attributes and yet avoid the kind of confusion such traditional
terms as "imagination" have been subject to? We need two terms
having special relevance to the poetic process and at the same
time reflecting the fundamental features of all human thought.
These terms must be so basic that they will describe mental
activity in all its variety—including the experience of poetry—
with a minimum of distortion. Psychoanalysis provides the appropriate concepts, which Freud named the "primary process"
and the "secondary process."[4]

The primary process and the secondary process are usually described as modes of energy discharge. Both modes of discharge
involve mental activity analogous to what we know as "thinking."
Indeed, it is common to speak of "primary-process thinking" and
"secondary-process thinking." The latter refers roughly to what is
ordinarily known as thinking, that is, to mental activity which is
conscious, reality-oriented, and more or less deliberate. But the
primary process, which may be unconscious, "unreal," and seemingly random or inadvertent, serves as the major vehicle for the
expression of ideas and emotions in such phenomena as dreams

3. The pioneering study of Frederick Clarke Prescott, *The Poetic Mind* (Ithaca:
Cornell University Press, 1959) attempts a division of thought somewhat similar
to the one I am proposing, but his categories, like "ordinary thought" versus
"poetic thought" (p. 53), lack conceptual precision.

4. Freud introduced these terms in his early (1895) *Project for a Scientific
Psychology: Std. Ed.* I, pp. 283-397. (Please note: all references to the work of
Freud are to *The Standard Edition of the Complete Psychological Works of
Sigmund Freud,* trans. James Strachey, Anna Freud, Alix Strachey, and Alan Tyson,
ed. James Strachey (London: Hogarth Press, 1966), 24 volumes, abbreviated here
and hereafter as *Std. Ed.*). See also Chapter VII of *The Interpretation of Dreams:
Std. Ed.* V, pp. 509-621. For a convenient introduction to these concepts, see
Robert Fliess, "On the Nature of Human Thought: The Primary and the Secondary Process as Exemplified by the Dream and Other Psychic Productions,"
reprinted in *Readings in Psychoanalytic Psychology,* ed. Morton Levitt (New
York: Appleton-Century-Crofts, 1959), pp. 213-20. For further guidance to psychoanalytic literature about these processes, see Robert Rogers, "On the Metapsychology of Poetic Language: Modal Ambiguity," *Int. J. Psycho-Anal.* 54 (1973):
61-74.

and hallucinations. Hence it is quite unlike what people ordinarily conceive thinking to be, so much so that I prefer to speak of "primary-process mentation" and "secondary-process mentation." The term "mentation" denotes mental activity without evoking the unwanted connotations of the word "thinking," which are only misleading in connection with the primary process.

The best way to begin explaining primary-process mentation is to specify the situations in which it is likely to come into play. It occurs most notably in dreams and may even be characterized as the language of dreams. It plays a major role in the mental activity of neurotics and psychotics. When the psychotic Dr. Schreber (Freud, "A Case of Paranoia," *Std. Ed.,* XII) develops a delusional philosophy involving the assumption that he has a mission to redeem the world and restore it to the state of bliss after being transformed into a woman and impregnated by God, he is employing the primary process. We may call his delusional system symptomatic and symbolic, but for him it has the status of literal fact. Temporary states of psychosis induced by chemicals (narcotics, including hallucinogens) and electric stimulation of the brain likewise give rise to primary process mentation.[5] The subject of a mescaline experiment claimed she knew what it felt like to be a table: "I could feel the sort of pressure where your legs join the table top. I could feel what it was like looking in all directions and not facing any way—being properly symmetrical as it were—a bit to do with being wood, and having been a tree."[6] States of alcoholic intoxication may liberate primary-process activity ranging from mild reverie to delirium tremens. Similarly, states of extreme emotion like rage ("anger is brief madness") and sexual orgasm may be accompanied by the primary process, as are physiological states of extreme deprivation, like exhaustion and thirst. A typical example is the hallucinated oasis of the man dying of thirst in a desert. Conditions of heightened sensitivity like the rapt ecstasy of the religious mystic's trance or the manic, inspirational phase of creative imagination involve pri-

5. For an account of the results of electrical stimulation of the brain on fantasy production, see Mardi J. Horowitz, "Visual Imagery and Cognitive Organization," *Amer. J. Psychiat.* 123 (February, 1967): 938-46.

6. See Peter McKeller, *Imagination and Thinking* (London: Cohen and West, 1957), p. 107.

mary-process mentation. To these instances might be added the period of relatively early childhood when the full range of mental activity has yet to develop. All of these situations have in common periods of reduced ego control, times when self-criticism and reality-testing are minimal or entirely absent.

There are a number of other characteristics common to the primary process besides its tendency to take over during periods of reduced ego control. The most striking of these is that it ignores considerations of time, space, and logical consistency, like a surrealist painting or a book like *Through the Looking-Glass* (the White Queen cries with pain *before* she pricks her finger because her memory works backwards). The primary process is magical and wishful, even to the point of sometimes expressing what is known as omnipotence of thought. This omnipotence involves the assumption that "thinking will make it so." It most often takes the negative form of a fear that a thought or deed will magically cause something to happen, as in the sidewalk ritual of children: "step on a crack, break your mother's back." For the most part, primary-process mentation is concrete, usually pictorial, as in dreams. It employs symbolism in a crudely associative way. This symbolism differs from what people usually consider symbolism in that similarities are not realized as mere similarities but treated as identities. Thus in Freudian iconography one encounters such typical equations as sword equals penis; box equals vagina; departure equals death; riding equals sexual intercourse; king equals father; and less obviously, money equals feces and body equals phallus. There is no point in the commonsensical objection that filthy lucre does not remotely resemble feces because the primary process pays no heed to common sense. That is one of its secret sources of power. It can equate almost anything with anything else where even the most rudimentary similarity exists, such as an isomorphic one. According to the primary process, the symbol equals reality: "Preconscious pictorial thinking is a magical type of thinking. The object and the idea of the object, the object and a picture or model of the object, the object and a part of the object are equated; similarities are not distinguished from identities; ego and nonego are not yet separated."[7]

7. Otto Fenichel, *The Psychoanalytic Theory of Neurosis* (New York: Norton, 1945), p. 47.

Three other peculiarities of the primary process may be mentioned here. It is regressive in the sense that it operates in the service of regressive impulses. It tends to be nonverbal or preverbal, and when it is expressed through the medium of words the diction remains primitive in certain ways, as will be clear later on. Finally, like Molly Bloom, the primary process never says no. To be more precise, only indirect representations of negation occur, as the following dream will illustrate. A man enters a haberdashery to buy a necktie only to be told to his amazement that he is already wearing several. The dreamer in this instance understood that the neckties were phallic but did not at first realize that the multiplication of phallic objects symbolized in a positive fashion a fantasied solution to the negative problem of castration anxiety.

At this point the primary process may be more fully differentiated from the secondary process. The primary process operates mainly in the service of the id as a mode of discharging free, mobile psychic energy. It employs a crude, analogical, associative form of symbolism in a magical, wishful fashion without regard for ordinary reality, time, space, and logical consistency. While the mentation itself may be conscious, its sources are apt to be dynamically repressed. The secondary process operates mainly in the service of the ego. The psychic energy at its disposal is bound, or neutralized, or sublimated energy. As a mode of expression it is rational, conceptual, analytical. It utilizes higher, more abstract forms of discourse such as conventional lexical language and standardized mathematical signs.

Freud's distinction between primary- and secondary-process mentation corresponds in many ways to the discrimination now commonly made in information theory between analog and digital communication. An analog computer operates on the basis of making comparisons of some kind between sets of categories which have something more or less similar in common, such as length or size; a digital computer operates by substitution, the substituted category being discontinuous and arbitrary rather than continuous and similar. Thus our male collie may be said to communicate analogically with other dogs by marking the "map" of his territory with urine in such a way that the size of the map corresponds to the size of the territory, but the word "dog" as I have just used it communicates digitally to the reader via an arbitrary lexical sign that has nothing dog-like about it in terms of size, shape, smell, hairiness, or whatever. Metaphor communicates both analogically and digitally. A metaphor digitally and rather arbitrarily says, "A this is a that" and always at the same time implies in a similaic, analogical way that "A this is *like* a that." When Othello declares, "Keep up your bright swords, for the dew will rust them," he speaks digitally to the extent that he speaks literally (since it is night, and so the dew is "falling") and yet Othello speaks analogically in appealing to the sense of honor of Brabantio's men by assuming certain correspondences between their honor and their bright swords. While it may prove useful on occasion to refer to analog and digital aspects of metaphor, the primary and secondary processes, being psychological terms, will normally be more congruent with my purposes.

What, then, is the relationship of the primary and secondary processes to poetry? How can an understanding of these fundamental modes of mentation be instrumental in discovering more about the nature of poetic language, particularly its effect on the reader? I can begin to answer these questions by suggesting that the poet makes extraordinary use of the primary process and that the principal vehicle of the mode is metaphor. By way of learning to recognize manifestations of the primary process in literature proper, it will be helpful to start by locating examples in the verbal genres of nursery rhyme and nonsense verse. Closer to sheer fantasy, they reveal the primary process in a relatively unadulterated way.

What is it that haunts us in the sad saga of the three blind mice?

> Three blind mice. Three blind mice.
> See how they run. See how they run.
> They all ran after the farmer's wife.
> She cut off their tails with a carving knife.
> Did you ever see such a sight in your life
> As three blind mice?

Funny or horrible, absurd or pitiful, in any case this barnyard tragedy transcends ordinary reality. Mice do not chase humans. Even if they did, blind ones could not run after the farmer's wife because they could not see to follow her. If she did not want them to run after her she would cut off their legs or heads—not their tails. Fantasy is what we have to do with, fantasy and mystery.

Why are the mice blind in the first place? Why are there three of them? Why do they chase the farmer's wife? At the level of the primary process the arbitrary features of the narration coalesce into meaning. The song has coherence, or what literary critics like to call "organic unity." If the number three has the same phallic implications it so often does elsewhere in myth and folklore, then the mice may be considered as a kind of "reverse synecdoche" where the whole of the body represents one of its parts—in this case the phallus. If this meaning applies here, then lust may be the motive of the mice. The motility theme of running expresses their lust. Their lust accounts for the farmer's wife's fear (or anger?). She punishes their sexual crime in an appropriate fashion by castrating rather than killing them. Their blindness symbolically reinforces or restates the nature of the punishment in the redundant manner typical of so much sexual symbolism in fantasy. And the fact that the woman happens to be the farmer's wife, or anyone's wife, suggests that she belongs to someone else sexually, adding an oedipal dimension to the story. Her aggressiveness also betokens her role as the pre-oedipal phallic mother.

With one exception, structural elements in the song seem to lend support to this interpretation. That the mice are blind to begin with, which is the exception, may be accounted for as the result of displacement (in narrative sequence); otherwise anti-cipated punishment follows fantasied crime in normal fashion. The emphatic three-beat rhythm of the first, second, and last lines duplicates the narrative element "three." The theme of vision and blindness as symbolic lust and castration continues from the first line, through the repeated imperative "see" in the second, to the emphasis on seeing an unusual sight in the penul-timate line. Throughout the poem, which is what it is by any reasonable criteria, the stress on seeing accomplishes the anti-dotal feat of reassuring the detached listener that since he can see the strange sight with his mind's eye, he himself is whole and hale, not having been subject to dismemberment. Even structure in the sense of genre becomes an element of meaning in that the song is a round, something continuous, that does not get cut off at the end the way an ordinary song does. The song succeeds with remarkable economy in generating, controlling, and dispelling anxiety.

Even if this interpretation enjoys a certain coherence and comprehensiveness, it may or may not accurately locate the sources of this song's popularity. In so brief a work it is difficult to establish contextual validation of the symbolism. Aside from a few narrative cues like the conventional sequence of crime and punishment, which is seldom reversed even in the time-ignoring patterns of the primary process, most of the cues come from the diction. It will be noticed that this plain and simple diction belongs to what Hawthorne calls "the humblest medium of familiar words and images." Of particular moment is the fact that many of the words refer either directly or symbolically to parts and functions of the body, one reason why many of the words are so familiar. Another aspect of the diction deserves mention. It appears to be literal without exception. Not a single conventional metaphor occurs within the poem. In actuality, most of the words of the poem belong to a species which I will call *naive metaphor,* to be explained shortly. As for the amount of information allegedly derived from the words of this poem, the incalculable richness of primary-process language as a vehicle of expression remains to be established.

Another nonsense poem saturated with the primary process is Lewis Carroll's "Jabberwocky":

> 'Twas brillig, and the slithy toves
> Did gyre and gimble in the wabe:
> All mimsy were the borogoves,
> And the mome raths outgrabe.

> "Beware the Jabberwock, my son!
> The jaws that bite, the claws that catch!
> Beware the Jubjub bird, and shun
> The frumious Bandersnatch!"

> He took his vorpal sword in hand:
> Long time the manxome foe he sought—
> So rested he by the Tumtum tree,
> And stood a while in thought.

> And, as in uffish thought he stood,
> The Jabberwock, with eyes of flame,
> Came whiffling through the tulgey wood,
> And burbled as it came!

> One, two! One, two! And through and through
> The vorpal blade went snicker-snack!
> He left it dead, and with its head
> He went galumphing back.

"And hast thou slain the Jabberwock?
Come to my arms, my beamish boy!
O frabjous day! Callooh! Callay!"
He chortled in his joy.

'Twas brillig, and the slithy toves
Did gyre and gimble in the wabe:
All mimsy were the borogoves,
And the mome raths outgrabe.

The language seems unfamiliar to Alice until she realizes it is
mirror-writing, yet even when held up to a mirror she finds it
hard to understand. Somehow it fills her head with ideas, "only I
don't exactly know what they are! However, *somebody* killed
something: that's clear at any rate." Humpty Dumpty, who claims
to be able to explain all the poems ever invented, including some
not yet written, free associates freely enough with the first stanza
but unaccountably halts his exegesis there, just where things get
interesting.

If I adopt some of Humpty Dumpty's critical arrogance, and
rely on his assumption that nonsense is not always nonsensical, I
can regard the hero as a psychological son who searches out a
castrating father figure ("the jaws that bite, the claws that catch")
in order to symbolically counter-castrate the ogre by beheading
him. He returns home with this paternal phallus to the arms of
the good, kind, unthreatening, asexual father figure. Tenniel's
priceless illustration of the waistcoated dragon reinforces the idea
that the psychological father has been split, or decomposed, into
fragments.[8] But instead of bothering to relate this oedipal romance to other elements in Carroll's work (like the danger that
Humpty Dumpty may lose his head if he smiles too hard, or the
probable difficulty of beheading the Cheshire Cat), I will limit
myself to pointing out certain features of the language of the
poem.

It ranges from simple, straightforward words like "jaws,"
"claws," "head," and "arms" to nonreferential phrases like
"mome raths outgrabe." Within these extremes occur suggestive,
sometimes onomatopoetic neologisms like "frumious," "burbled,"
"snicker-snack," and "beamish." Except for the framing stanzas,

---

8. For an extended discussion of decomposition, see Robert Rogers, *A Psychoanalytic Study of the Double in Literature* (Detroit: Wayne State University Press,
1970).

there is enough simple prose statement, like "He left it dead," to cement the various parts into a relatively coherent narrative. What we have, in short, is not nonsense verse but meaningful verse disguised as nonsense verse, or sense interlarded with nonsense. The framing stanzas, composed of almost but not quite pure nonsense, function in such a way as to throw the reader off his guard by mesmerically inducing him to abandon reality-testing in order to participate more fully and without criticism in the emotionally loaded material of the poem proper. Nonsensical elements appearing within the poem proper and within the larger framework of Alice's adventures in the land through the looking-glass perform the same function. In contrast to the more intellectualized defenses of most literature, the genre of nonsense uses the simple tactic of disguising potentially disturbing fantasy as harmless nonsense in much the same way that the element of absurdity in dreams serves a defensive purpose. In short, "Jabberwocky" entices us into the magical, primitive, make-believe realm of the primary process by the disarming strategy of assuring us it cannot be taken seriously. Communication takes place in an astonishingly effective way but not at conscious levels. The primary process as a channel of communication is in many ways equal—and in some superior—to that of the secondary process, but the messages are encoded in a different way. Lewis Carroll addresses the whole human brotherhood "in the heart's native language," exactly the medium Dimmesdale uses to communicate with his congregation. Both employ a code "understood" at levels below consciousness. Because it involves modalities of communication which for the most part transcend barriers of language and culture, concrete imagery "containing" a large proportion of primary-process mentation translates easily from one tongue to another. I assume, for example, that Clytemnestra's dream of giving birth to a snake which bites her breast when she nurses it loses little or no psychological meaning in translation.

These two poems convey most of their meaning through the medium of naive metaphors (words with fairly concrete referents which appear to be literal but which attain a metaphoric dimension by effecting a symbolic transfer, usually an unconscious one). When Turbayne remarks, "It is a mistake to present the facts of one sort in the idioms of another *without awareness*," he has in mind the dangers of using metaphor unintentionally in scientific

discourse.[9] His statement naturally does not hold for the kind
of symbolic discourse we encounter in myth and fairy tale. At the
narrative level Prometheus steals real fire from heaven and Little
Red Riding Hood actually gets gobbled up by the wolf, though at
a symbolic level the fire may be libidinal and the incorporation
may reflect a childlike confusion about the nature of sexual
intercourse. I call metaphors which are not intended as metaphors "naive" because they are childlike. Young children often
take the figurative expressions of adults literally. At the age of
four my son became frightened when I remarked casually of some
domestic issue, "Your mother will kill me if. . . ." Yet as Norman
Holland paraphrases, "Except ye become as little children, ye
shall not enter the kingdom of literature."[10] Just as ego psychology speaks of the artist's "flexibility of repression" and his
"regression in the service of the ego," so must there take place a
comparable regression on the part of the reader as he responds
to fiction as though it were fact. At the same time he responds to
fictional nonmetaphors like the Jabberwock's jaws as though they
were actual jaws, he simultaneously treats these objects as metaphors by making the appropriate unconscious associations or
transfers. In other words, there is no important psychological
difference between the reader's response to the Jabberwock's
"eyes of flame," a conventional metaphor, and his response to
"jaws that bite," a naive metaphor. I said earlier that metaphor is
the principal outlet for the expression of primary-process mentation in literature. It will now be clear that much apparently literal
verbal detail also expresses primary-process mentation if it belongs to the category of naive metaphor.

It is worth noticing, to return to the question of Coleridge's
two modes of thought, that Lowes compares the composition of
"The Rime of the Ancient Mariner" and "Kubla Khan" by saying
that "the complicating factor—the will as a conscious construc-
tive agency—was in abeyance" when "Kubla Khan" was written.[11] Another way of describing the difference would be to say

    9. Colin M. Turbayne, *The Myth of Metaphor* (New Haven: Yale University
Press, 1962), p. 22.
    10. Norman N. Holland, *The Dynamics of Literary Response* (New York:
Oxford University Press, 1968), p. 80.
    11. Lowes, *Road to Xanadu,* p. 401.

that in "The Ancient Mariner" we encounter the mixture of primary and secondary process material normal in most literature but that in "Kubla Khan" we have an example of what is close to being pure primary process—which is exactly what we might expect to find in view of the circumstances under which it was written. While Elisabeth Schneider has shown in *Coleridge, Opium, and Kubla Khan* that the exact circumstances of its composition remain in doubt, it does not matter whether Coleridge fell into a state of sleep after taking a dose of opium and subsequently transcribed a dream episode upon awakening or whether he simply composed the poem during a narcotic-induced reverie. What does matter in the present context is that the dream-like language and atmosphere announce the poem's primary process character, as this portion reveals:

> In Xanadu did Kubla Khan
> A stately pleasure-dome decree:
> Where Alph, the sacred river, ran
> Through caverns measureless to man
> Down to the sunless sea.
> So twice five miles of fertile ground
> With walls and towers were girdled round:
> And here were gardens bright with sinuous rills
> Where blossomed many an incense-bearing tree;
> And here were forests ancient as the hills,
> Enfolding sunny spots of greenery.
> But oh! that deep romantic chasm which slanted
> Down the green hill athwart a cedarn cover!
> A savage place! as holy and enchanted
> As e'er beneath a waning moon was haunted
> By woman wailing for her demon-lover!
> And from this chasm, with ceaseless turmoil seething,
> As if this earth in fast thick pants were breathing,
> A mighty fountain momently was forced;
> Amid whose swift half-intermitted burst
> Huge fragments vaulted like rebounding hail,
> Or chaffy grain beneath the thresher's flail.

An orthodox Freudian interpreter might point to the common dream symbolism of the body-as-landscape, suggest that the activity occurring in the "savage place" resembles coition and probably represents a primal scene, and propose that the "he" of the end of the fragment who has fed on "honey-dew" and "drunk the milk of Paradise" prefers the oral satisfactions of the pleasure-dome to the imagined coldness of vaginal "caves of ice." But this reading is highly inferential. The text confronts the would-be interpreter with enormous difficulties, including the insuperable one of being a fragment, not a complete poem, so that the total context of the organic whole can never be established as a check on interpretation, though several psychological analyses have nevertheless been advanced.[12]

My remarks at the moment must be confined to the general character of the language of "Kubla Khan." I can think of no other work that manifests the primary process with so little leavening of the cognitive element and yet has been accorded such high rank as poetry, though the esteem in which it is held might not be so great if people did not know Coleridge wrote it. He claimed he published it "rather as a psychological curiosity, than on the ground of any supposed *poetic* merits." The special character of its language can be dramatized by contrasting it with the high proportion of secondary-process language in a passage from *Joan of Arc,* a dreadful botch on which Coleridge collaborated with Southey:

> But Properties are God: the naked mass
> Acts only by its inactivity.
> Here we pause humbly. Others boldlier think
> That as one body is the aggregate
> Of atoms numberless, each organiz'd;
> So by a strange and dim similitude,
> Infinite myriads of self-conscious minds
> Form one all-conscious Spirit, who directs
> With absolute ubiquity of thought
> All his component monads, that yet seem
> With various province and apt agency
> Each to pursue its own self-centering end.
>
> [Bk. II, 38-49]

12. See especially Eli Marcovitz, "Bemoaning the Lost Dream: Coleridge's 'Kubla Khan' and Addiction," *Int. J. Psycho-Anal.* 45 (1964): 411-25, and Kenneth Burke, " 'Kubla Khan,' Proto-Surrealist Poem," in *Language as Symbolic Action* (Berkeley: University of California Press, 1966), pp. 201-202. Burke suggests the poem traces "in terms of imagery the very *form* of thinking. . . . It is as though, like Kantian transcendentalism, Coleridge were speculating epistemologically on the nature of consciousness." See also James F. Hoyle, " 'Kubla Khan' as an Elated Experience," *Literature and Psychology* 16 (1967): 27-39, and Eugene H. Sloane, "Coleridge's *Kubla Khan*: The Living Catacombs of the Mind," *American Imago* 29 (Summer, 1972): 97-122.

The language of this passage is almost exclusively of the secondary-process variety. Coleridge later commented on the absence of "all Bone, Muscle, and Sinew in the single Lines" of the poem, which certainly does not employ the humblest medium of familiar words and images. Though the language is appropriate to the subject matter, the passage represents metaphysics poeticized, not poetry. Latinate and conceptual, the diction spends its force in sterile abstractions. Even the word "body" is abstract in context, and a phrase like "naked mass," without psychological underpinnings, has the feel of a dead metaphor. By comparison, the richly concrete language of "Kubla Khan" radiates emotion and floods us with associations, however random and confused, although a small proportion of its diction is ideational and abstract enough to belong in the secondary-process category (words like "sacred," "measureless," "romantic," "holy," and "half-intermitted ").

With these samples in mind it may now be asked if it is at all accurate to talk of primary- and secondary-process language. Strictly speaking, there is no such thing as a primary-process word. When such phraseology occurs it should be understood as an expository convenience for expressing the idea that certain words in certain contexts have potential for mobilizing primary- or secondary-process mentation—as the case may be—in the reader. In other words, primary-process diction may be said to partake of the characteristics of the primary process: it is primitive, impulse-laden, id-oriented, wishfulfilling, hallucinatory, concrete, symbolic diction, diction which may paradoxically be said to have a preverbal quality. Secondary-process words are "adult words." They tend to be abstract, have a defensive function, and be ego and superego oriented. They appeal to the conscious mind for the most part. They are geared to problem-solving, reality-testing cognition. Abstract, conceptual words like "world," "nature," and "soul" tend to fall into this category, though schizophrenics often use such words in a primary-process fashion. Less common, polysyllabic, "literary" words like "primeval" also involve the secondary process. Unlike the free, mobile energy-infusing primary-process diction, secondary-process diction utilizes what Freud thought of as bound, neutralized psychic energy.

It should be realized that primary-process language never occurs in pure form. Just as it is common to assume in literary criticism that elements of form and content cannot be separated, neither can the primary- and secondary-components of an image or metaphor be distinguished with scientific rigor by some kind of fractional distillation. It will eventually be shown, however, that for analytical purposes certain useful presumptions may be formed as to the type and degree of mentation a given word or phrase *in a particular context* will express or generate. This possibility provides in turn a framework within which the full range of the dynamics of the reader's response to language can be described in terms of the interaction of primary- and secondary-process mentation.

At this point it would be helpful to have a simple, relatively concrete term to use as a scientific model providing a locus of reference for further explanation. In physics the wave and photon theories of the behavior of light have such a function, as do concepts like drive and defense in psychoanalysis. For my purposes the idea of verbal tension will serve. As I indicated, many critics think of metaphorical language as involving some kind of dynamic process which creates "tension" between words or clusters of words. Assuming they are on the right track, it may be supposed that poetic language, at its best, exercises a kind of push-pull or repulsion-attraction on the mind of the reader which he remains largely unaware of, the diction seeming "good" or "beautiful" or "enthralling" or "profound" in direct proportion to the differential between the "push" and the "pull." But this simplistic mechanical notion of verbal tension needs to be explained in more precise conceptual language for much the same reason that scientific models like waves and photons, which are not theories but kernels of theories, can only be described with precision by having recourse to higher mathematics.

A psychological theory of poetic language may be stated with some gain in precision by elaborating on the tension model as follows. *Under certain contextual conditions language mobilizes primary- and secondary-process mentation in the reader in such a way that endopsychic tension develops, a passage being felt as vital or powerful or imaginative in proportion to the amount of tension generated between drive and defense structures—includ-*

ing memory structures and identity configurations. The primary and secondary processes are not the direct source of tension but rather the media or matrices through which the opposing forces of drive and defense are mobilized. Pleasure derived from experiencing such language probably results more from modulation of the mentational forms than from simple arousal or discharge of tension. This model, a homeostatic one, does not require the theoretically awkward assumption of the discharge of large amounts of energy. On the contrary, it assumes gratification to be based on a controlled variation or articulation of homeostatic shifts of the cathected (emotionally charged) contents of memory systems[13] Another way of viewing this model that obviates the assumption of drive energy is to regard emotions attached to specific memories as constituting potential feedback in a self-regulating homeostatic system. If the reader of a text be regarded as constituting such a system, then any emotions he experiences in the course of reading amount to a form of informational feedback within his Self-System—including that preposterous tangle of memory, impulse, and inhibition we call Personality, or Identity.

One of the smallest linguistic entities promoting such homeostatic shifts in the reader's cognitive and emotional equilibrium is metaphor. Every metaphor presents us with a tiny puzzle, as Aristotle has it. I can put the matter another way by suggesting that every "labelled" metaphor presents the reader with a "mini-bind," or minimal double bind, to use the formulation of Gregory Bateson and his colleagues.[14] In other words, every metaphor contains a built-in falsification of logical types, a built-in invitation to read its message in at least two different and more-or-less incompatible ways, as in "Blind mouths!"—the catachresis Milton employs in "Lycidas" as an image for greedy churchmen. Similarly, every metaphor contains a built-in violation of reality-testing, though one difference between poetry and the language of a schizophrenogenic mother is that poetic metaphors are always accompanied by meta-communicational messages saying,

13. Cf. Peter L. Giovacchini, *Tactics and Techniques in Psychoanalytic Therapy* (New York: Science House, Inc., 1972), pp. 140-41.

14. Gregory Bateson et al., "Toward a Theory of Schizophrenia," *Behavioral Science* 1 (1956): 250-64.

"Treat all these messages as as-ifs; treat them as deliberate falsi-
fications in the service of whatever truths poetry has to offer. Do
not confuse these messages with reality in the ordinary sense."
Tensions set up by this kind of double-binding in poetic language
may be need-satisfying as long as the reader understands the
meta-communicational frame of reference.

The psychological theory of response to language I am proposing may prove confusing unless the status of "tension" as a
meta-metaphor is kept in mind. Anatol Rapoport says of the role
of metaphor in scientific models that "exact science is characterized, then, not by the absence of metaphor but by their abun-
dant use with full recognition of their limitations. Scientific
metaphors are called 'models.' "[15] They are made with full awareness that the relationship between the metaphor and what it
represents exists primarily in the mind of the scientist. There is
an "as-if-ness" about scientific models, says Rapoport, which
"insulates" the model from reality, preventing a false identification of the two. Thus scientific metaphors are pragmatic devices,
discardable after they prove unfruitful. As for the value of such
models, Frederick Crews reminds us that the strength of psychoanalysis lies in the relative precision of its metaphors, that is, in
"their capacity for economically describing a vast range of evidence for which no other descriptive terms have been found."[16]

Since the two modes of mentation in poetry have been illustrated thus far only by rather anomalous examples, I will make
the first direct application of the tension model to poetry of
unquestionable merit: Cleopatra's speech as she contemplates
suicide.

> My desolation does begin to make
> A better life. 'Tis paltry to be Caesar.
> Not being Fortune, he's but Fortune's knave,
> A minister of her will. And it is great
> To do that thing that ends all other deeds,
> Which shackles accidents and bolts up change,
> Which sleeps, and never palates more the dug,
> The beggar's nurse and Caesar's.
>
> [*Ant.* 5.2.1-8]

15. Anatol Rapoport, *Operational Philosophy* (New York: John Wiley & Sons,
1965), p. 206.

16. Frederick Crews, "Literature and Psychology," in *Relations of Literary*

One eminent editor—a scrupulous observer of textual variations
—notes that in place of "dug" the First Folio reads "dung." If
"dung" is the original word, he argues, then the passage means,
"Death makes us sleep and never more eat the dung (i.e., food
grown out of manure), which nourishes alike a beggar and a
Caesar."[17] Such a reading, he claims, echoes Antony's "our dungy
earth alike feeds beast and man" (1.1.35-36) and reflects "morbid
broodings on the various transmutations of matter" common in
the early seventeenth century. There is nothing innately ridiculous in this reading, despite appearances. Final determinations
about the authenticity of Shakespearean texts are often impossible to make, and Shakespeare could mix metaphors as no one
ever could. Yet this editor's reading may stem more from schol-
arly zeal than critical judgment. The line of Antony's almost
literally elaborates the metaphor immediately preceding it,
"Kingdom's are clay," and Antony's theme in Act I seems to be
not life or death or equality but the *nobility* of a life great love and
vast kingdoms make for. As for the context of Cleopatra's speech,
the dug image coincides better with the profoundly stirring lines
she utters later on as she puts the asp to her breast:

> Peace, peace!
> Dost thou not see my baby at my breast,
> That sucks the nurse to sleep?

However abrupt and unexpected the image of Death as a dug may
be, it does not sprain the joints of the reader's mind the way
linking "dung" with "nurse" and "sleep" would require.

Middleton Murry gives a helpful interpretation of Cleopatra's
speech.[18] After comparing the mixed metaphors of a modern
poet to what only appear to be mixed ones in Shakespeare's
passage, Murry says, "We have not, and we are not intended to
have, time to unfold his metaphors; and, moreover, the boldest
and most abrupt transition among them is in its effect the
smoothest. For the rhythm leaves no doubt that it is not 'the dug'

Study, ed. James Thorpe (New York: Modern Language Association of America,
1967), p. 77.
  17. George B. Harrison, in his *Shakespeare: The Complete Works* (New York:
Harcourt, Brace, 1948), p. 1260.
  18. John Middleton Murry, "Metaphor," in *Countries of the Mind,* pp. 5-7.

but Death that is 'the beggar's nurse and Caesar's.' " Murry adds
that Death, "the child sleeping against the heart" in the penul-
timate line, becomes in the last line "the bosom that receives
mankind." While Murry's reading captures much of the richness
of the passage, and while Death becomes "the beggar's nurse and
Caesar's," I would submit that Murry has no call to insist that the
dug is not as well. We can have the dug metaphor both ways.

Assuming, then, that Shakespeare intended the dug metaphor,
I imagine the reader's probable response to Cleopatra's remarks
runs something like this. Surcharged with irony, the passage
forces the reader's mind to concentrate in a highly conscious way
on the implications of several paradoxes. Desolation makes for a
better life, which is death, and constitutes a beginning, which is
an end. It is paltry to be great, that is, Caesar, an emperor who is
only fortune's knave. Then Cleopatra moves from emotional
thought to thoughtful emotion. She and the reader plunge from
lofty metaphysical speculation involving conceptual thought of a
high order down to the more concrete level of "shackles acci-
dents and bolts up change," and from there to the ultimate
simplicity: the dug—elemental source and symbol of life. The
shift here is from secondary to primary process, though the dug
image sustains both modes. In this passage the beggar's nurse and
Caesar's is death, and death becomes in the last two lines, as
Murry says, "the bosom that receives mankind." But the dug of
life is also the beggar's nurse and Caesar's, reiterating the equality
motif in the play by showing that all men begin life at the same
place regardless of their later social status and likewise end at the
same place: the dug of death. Suicide, and hence death, "which
sleeps, and never palates more the dug," implies a sempiternal
death that never allows any return to suck the dug of life. Surfeit at
the literal dug of life leads the nursing infant to a blissful sleep, but
the figurative dug of death provides a better, longer sleep after
the surfeit of a lifetime of pleasure, including the kind of pleasurable death alluded to elsewhere in the play, as when Enobarbus
praises Cleopatra's "celerity in dying" (sexually) and when Antony says, as he falls on his sword:

> But I will be
> A bridegroom in my death, and run into it
> As to a lover's bed.

The poetry of Cleopatra's suicide speech obliges us to prefer, in imagination, the wizened breast of death to the plump one of life.

Thus the image of the dug mobilizes our deepest, most primitive impulses in a context completely antithetical to them. A tensive response grows out of the dramatized antithesis of drive objects. Readers can experience this profound conflict as a pleasurable homeostasis because of the control Shakespeare exercises over his material (inducing a temporary illusion of the ego's ability to master dangerous inner impulses and outer forces) and because most of the conflict remains unconscious. Massive appeal to secondary-process ideation constitutes the principal medium of defense (intellectualization as defense). To be sure, the tension-producing conflict I have hypothesized cannot be weighed or measured or pointed to directly. Though it can only be inferred, a crude demonstration of its invisible presence can be made by the simple experiment of altering the last two lines to read

> Which sleeps, and dreams, in that same bed
> Where Caesar and the beggar's nurse do lie.

This change yanks most of the orality from the lines. While much of the more superficial meaning of the passage remains, deeper associations like that of sleep with surfeit-at-the-breast disappear. Substituting a grave image for the dug image actually increases the immediate comprehensibility of the lines but only at the cost of wrenching out of them all the dramatic antithesis of the associations with life and death Shakespeare's imagery foments within us.

The tension model applies equally well if one looks at the tension hypothetically generated by the dug metaphor in terms of object relations. So regarded, poetic imagery restores the lost object—here the original lost object, the breast. Poetry restores the lost object, momentarily at least, in a much more general and pervasive way than this particular example would imply. David Bleich argues that the original motive for the acquisition of language is to be able to deal with the sense of affective loss consequent upon the departure of a loved person or the loss of a transitional object such as Freud depicts in the *fort—da!* game his grandson plays in his crib with the aid of some string and a spool.[19]

19. David Bleich, "New Considerations of the Infantile Acquisition of Language and Symbolic Thought," *Psychoanalytic Review* 63 (Spring, 1976): 57.

Language "represents to the child a *way back* to the missing libidinal object," says Bleich. I am suggesting this statement holds for adults as well, in which connection I would emphasize the way primary-process mentation depends on a drive organization of memory traces; that is, by its very nature the primary process deals in drive-laden material.[20] Here, then, is the essential basis for all the nurturance of poetic language: it marshals unconscious memories of early losses, we experience a degree of intrapsychic tension as a result, and we more or less simultaneously obtain gratification—a substitute gratification, to be sure—by *taking in* the images the poet feeds us, as in the case, let us say, of these lines from Keats's "Ode to a Nightingale":

> O for a beaker full of the warm South
> Full of the true, the blushful Hippocrene,
> With beaded bubbles winking at the brim,
> And purple-stained mouth;
> That I might drink, and leave the world unseen,
> And with thee fade away into the forest dim.

Reading these lines presumably creates a sense of deprivation in us by inciting the represented wish and simultaneously fulfills this wish with the rich succor of Keats's imagery.

Before presenting a fuller illustration of the homeostatic model of reader response than I give in the example from Cleopatra's speech, I should like to consider some commentary suggesting the need for such a model.

William Empson's seventh type of ambiguity occurs when "the two meanings of the word, the two values of the ambiguity, are the two opposite meanings defined by the context, so that the total effect is to show a fundamental division of the writer's mind."[21] At one point Empson uses Hopkins's "The Windhover" as an example of indecision in the mind of the author. After remarking that certain lines reveal "a clear case of the Freudian use of opposites, where two things [are] thought of as incompatible, but desired intensely by different systems of judgment,"

---

20. See Hartvig Dahl, "Observations on a 'Natural Experiment': Helen Keller," *J. American Psychoanal. Assn.* 13 (1965): 548.

21. William Empson, *Seven Types of Ambiguity* (New York: New Directions, n.d.), p. 192.

Empson goes on to say this: "Such a process, one might imagine, could pierce to regions that underlie the whole structure of our thought; could tap energies of the very depths of the mind" (p. 226). My concern here is not with Empson's analysis of a particular kind of ambiguity in "The Windhover" but with the revolutionary generalization just quoted. He speaks of the possibility of a verbal process which could, rather like nuclear fission, tap untold sources of power. His statement hints at an emotion-thought dichotomy analogous to the primary-secondary process dichotomy. It emphasizes response to ambiguous language as a process experienced by the reader and indicates the enormous potential range of the dynamics of this process, which would presumably include unconscious response ("the very depths of the mind"). What the analysis of Cleopatra's suicide speech aims at is the elucidation of just such a process as Empson mentions, a process which can pierce the underlying regions of our thought and tap wellsprings of feeling at the very depths of the mind.

Ernest Fenellosa claims that poetry "must appeal to emotions with the charm of a direct impression, flashing through regions where the intellect can only grope," suggesting the way poetry appeals to a full spectrum of mental process.[22] "The best poetry," he adds, "deals not only with natural images but with lofty thoughts, spiritual suggestions and obscure relations." Thus the range of mentational dynamics must include ideas, which will naturally be expressed through the secondary process. A remark of Philip Wheelwright argues for an extreme range in what I am calling mentational dynamics: "What really matters in a metaphor is the psychic depth at which the things of the world, whether actual or fancied, are transmuted by the cool head of the imagination."[23] Owen Barfield, speaking of the transience of our response to the poetic moment, explains its ephemerality by saying the principal cause "appears to be that poetic experience depends on a 'difference of potential,' a kind of discrepancy between two modes or moods of consciousness. It is from this point, I take it, that a profitable study of the *psychology* of

22. Ernest Fenellosa, "The Chinese Written Character as a Medium for Poetry," in *Prose Keys to Modern Poetry,* ed. Karl Shapiro (New York: Harper & Row, 1962), pp. 147-48.

23. Philip Wheelwright, *Metaphor and Reality* (Bloomington: Indiana University Press, 1962), p. 71.

aesthetics would diverge."[24] If the term "mentation" is substituted for "consciousness," Barfield's remarks correspond closely to the tension model I am describing.

For Coleridge the ideal poet is one who can bring "the whole soul of man into activity."[25] In psychological terms, this formulation suggests the fullest possible range of mental activity. The power of the poet to blend, or fuse, or synthesize disparate entities into some kind of unity reveals itself, says Coleridge, in "the balance or reconciliation of opposite or discordant qualities," including "the idea with the image" and "a more than usual state of emotion with more than usual order." Such a balancing of discordant qualities can be discussed with relative precision in terms of interplay between the primary and secondary processes. Just prior to the remarks quoted above, Coleridge speaks of the kind of response a good poem will evoke as a whole: "The reader should be carried forward, not merely or chiefly by the mechanical impulse of curiosity, or by a restless desire to arrive at the final solution; but by the pleasurable activity of the mind excited by the attractions of the journey itself," a statement indicating that responding to the texture of poetic language involves a *process* to be experienced as an ongoing state of mental excitation rather than simply as the perception of a collection of verbal fragments which do no more than lead to some larger point or meaning. In connection with the two modes of mentation implied in Coleridge's mention of "the streamy nature of association, which thinking curbs and rudders," it is worth noting that Coleridge speaks in Chapter I of the *Biographia* of having learned "that poetry, even that of the loftiest and, seemingly, that of the wildest odes, had a logic of its own as severe as that of science." Much the same thing can be said of the primary process. It has a logic, an order, an economy, and a pattern of its own, however different from that of ordinary thought. In general, the more we know about how the mind works, the more we can understand the movement of poetry. As Lionel Trilling elegantly puts it, "Freudian psychology is the one which makes poetry indigenous to the very constitution of the mind. Indeed, the mind, as Freud sees it,

24. Owen Barfield, *Poetic Diction* (New York: McGraw-Hill, 1964), p. 54.
25. Samuel Taylor Coleridge, *Biographia Literaria*, ed. George B. Watson (London: J. M. Dent, 1965), p. 173.

is in the greater part of its tendency exactly a poetry-making organ."[26]

For further insight into the mind as a poetry-making organ, I turn for a moment to a group of analysts, clinicians, and analytically oriented critics. Ella Freeman Sharpe was the first analyst to give explicit attention to the role of metaphor in therapy, though much of what she says is of course implicit in earlier psychoanalytic work. In a paper entitled "Psycho-Physical Problems Revealed in Language: An Examination of Metaphor," she focuses on the way metaphoric statements like "I am sodden with despair" can refer back to conflictful situations like bedwetting in a patient's life.[27] Attention to ontogenic implications of such expressions helps to guide the analyst's therapeutic efforts. In addition to such clinical remarks the paper offers several interesting theoretical observations. "Words both reveal and conceal thought and emotion," says Sharpe, and she adds, "Metaphor fuses sense experience and thought in language. The artist fuses them in a material medium or in sounds with or without words." (Compare Coleridge's emphasis on fusion.) Sharpe stresses the physical basis from which metaphorical speech springs: "My theory is that metaphor can only evolve in language or in the arts when the bodily orifices become controlled." This hypothesis calls our attention to the way language so often expresses the modal concerns of early psychosexual phases, especially the pre-oedipal ones. Sharpe notes that words may express feeling without thought, thought without feeling, and—in the case of metaphor—a compromise formation involving the operations of id, ego, and superego. She also remarks on the extent to which choice of words is predetermined, or overdetermined, as in the case of slips of the tongue. She concludes, "Metaphor, then, is personal and individual even though the words and the phrases used are not of the speaker's coinage."

Mark Kanzer addresses himself to the individual elements metaphor reveals in "Autobiographical Aspects of the Writer's Imagery."[28] Undaunted by the common assumption that a writ-

26. Lionel Trilling, "Freud and Literature," in *Psychoanalysis and Literature,* ed. Hendrik M. Ruitenbeck (New York: Dutton, 1964), p. 266.

27. Ella Freeman Sharpe, in *Collected Papers on Psycho-Analysis,* ed. Marjorie Brierley (London: Hogarth Press, 1950), pp. 155-58.

28. Mark Kanzer, *Int. J. Psycho-Anal.* 40 (1959): 52-58.

er's work cannot be approached psychoanalytically if his free associations cannot be elicited, Kanzer maintains that reservoirs of autobiographical material may be tapped by examining a writer's imagery with sufficient care. Patterns of imagery peculiar to a given writer are in effect almost as individualistic as the curls and whorls of a man's fingerprints, though Kanzer does not use this comparison. Drawing on studies of constellations of imagery by Caroline Spurgeon, Edward A. Armstrong, and John Livingston Lowes, Kanzer makes a strong case for attending to configurations of imagery in a writer's work. Another paper by Kanzer of even greater theoretical interest emphasizes the tendency of patients to regress from ideational statements to imagery at moments of resistance during free association: "Basically, in such interplay between imagery and ideation, we are dealing with normal mental activity as it fluctuates between the primary and secondary processes, between the search for identity of perceptions and identity of ideas. . . . Free association, by encouraging suspension of the secondary processes, promotes the substitution of imagery for ideas."[29] These observations underline the concealing and revealing aspects of metaphor Sharpe speaks of. Applied to metaphor, the idea can be stated this way: the primary-process features of metaphor have the property of giving freer expression to drives by virtue of their inherent concealing power. Metaphors are rather like the wooden horse the Greeks gave the Trojans, not because they are necessarily destructive in nature (though in certain contexts imagery can exert this kind of power) but in the more limited sense that we take them in without suspecting the forces they contain.

Clinical interest in imagery seems to be on the increase, especially with respect to the way interpreting and otherwise utilizing a patient's metaphors provides a communicational bridge between patient and therapist that makes contact-at-a-suitable-distance easier to establish.[30] Some impressive clinical work has been done employing an uncovering procedure called "free imag-

29. Mark Kanzer, "Image Formation During Free Association," *Psychoanalytic Quarterly* 27 (1958): 475.

30. See, for example, Elaine Caruth and Rudolf Ekstein, "Interpretation within the Metaphor," *American Academy of Child Psychiatry Journal* 5 (1966): 35-45; and Norman Reider, "Metaphor as Interpretation," *Int. J. Psycho-Anal.* 53 (1972): 463-69.

ery," a technique analogous to free association.[31] This procedure
builds on a practice Freud tried but soon abandoned, that of
having patients close their eyes as they free associate. The free
imagery technique, regarded as adjunctive to psychoanalytically
oriented therapy rather than a substitute for it, encourages the
patient to report mental imagery in order to facilitate access to
primary-process mentation and discourage defensive verbalization. In his account of attention to imagery in contemporary
research and clinical work, Jerome L. Singer goes so far as to
suggest that because Freud was unduly suspicious of the value of
fantasy processes he may have erred "in not insisting on imagery
alone rather than allowing patients to shift to free *verbal* association."[32] Singer points to the widespread assumption of the inherent therapeutic value of having patients actively explore the
flow of their own images. The idea, one not really alien to
psychoanalysis proper, is that the patient needs to be trained to
be a patient reader of his own self-generated and self-generating
text.

To turn to psychoanalytically oriented literary theory bearing
on these assumptions about the dynamics of imagery, Simon O.
Lesser notes the close resemblance of the primary process and the
language of fictional works.[33] He says that fiction speaks a
language "more natural to us, more intimate, more readily understood, than our native tongue"—the heart's native language, as
Hawthorne calls it. Lesser notes that "the concrete, sensory
language of fiction single-handedly fosters the kind of anxiety-
free perception toward which form strives: it quickly and effectively transmits almost any kind of material without requiring

31. Joseph Reyher, "Free Imagery: An Uncovering Procedure," *J. Clinical
Psych.* 19 (1963): 454-59; also Joseph Reyher and William Smeltzer, "Uncovering
Properties of Visual Imagery and Verbal Association: A Comparative Study," *J.
Abnormal Psych.* 73 (1968): 218-22.

32. Jerome L. Singer, "The Vicissitudes of Imagery in Research and Clinical
Use," *Contemporary Psychoanalysis* 7 (Fall, 1971): 165. For a full account of
recent research and practice, see Singer's *Imagery and Daydream Methods in
Psychotherapy and Behavior Modification* (New York: Academic Press, 1974).
For an in-depth account of the work of a single practitioner, see Joseph E. Shorr,
Psychotherapy Through Imagery (New York: Intercontinental Medical Book
Corp., 1974).

33. Simon O. Lesser, *Fiction and the Unconscious* (New York: Vintage, 1962),
chapter 6.

the reader to put what he understands into words," so that, though composed of words, fiction's language becomes an instrument of nondiscursive communication.[34] Though Lesser has the language of prose fiction in mind, his remarks apply *a fortiori* to poetry.

In *Psychoanalysis and Shakespeare* Norman N. Holland reviews the relatively few psychological studies of Shakespeare's diction and imagery, and concludes that more attention needs to be paid to the "interaction" of words. In *The Dynamics of Literary Response* he asserts that concepts like orality and anality "lead us directly to images, which are, for the literary critic, probably his richest source of insight."[35] In the latter book Holland devotes a chapter, "The Displacement to Language," to showing some of the ways certain features of language contribute to managing or controlling fantasy elements in literature, especially sound factors like assonance, consonance, rhythm, and rhyme. My own stress on the mentational dynamics of metaphor assumes the importance of Holland's attention to the larger dichotomies of drive and defense, fantasy and form, and fantasy and meaning as sources of the reader's response to literature. I am of course fully aware that Holland's recent work makes elaborate departures from the position mapped out in his *Dynamics of Literary Response*.[36]

It will be apparent that my emphasis on metaphor corresponds closely with Norman O. Brown's. Some of my views of poetic language differ from his, however. No one accords a more important role to metaphor and the primary process in art than Brown, but Brown's prescription for poetry and culture would have us abandon the reality principle. Because he understands the richness of infantile sexuality, he clings to it, and because he recognizes the vitality of primitive elements in poetic language, he would rule everything else out. Brown celebrates the body of love and the love of body in poetry. Unlike Ella Freeman Sharpe, who stresses the ability of metaphor to reveal *and* conceal (and whose

34. Ibid., p. 153; his italics omitted.

35. Norman N. Holland, *Psychoanalysis and Shakespeare* (New York: McGraw-Hill, 1966), pp. 121-26; *The Dynamics of Literary Response* (New York: Oxford University Press, 1968), p. 34.

36. Norman N. Holland, *Poems in Persons* (New York: Norton, 1973) and *5 Readers Reading* (New Haven: Yale University Press, 1975).

work Brown cites repeatedly), Brown would strip the Muse to her body bare—and concealment be damned.

Some minor inaccuracies mar Brown's otherwise splendid discussion of the relationships between Eros and language in *Life Against Death*. When he mentions that "the technique of art, so radically different from the technique of science and rational discourse, is rooted in what Freud called the primary process— the procedures of the unconscious," he distorts the nature of the primary process by implying that the manifestations of it are entirely unconscious.[37] Speaking of metaphor as "the building block of all poetry," Brown asserts that metaphor "is nothing but a playing with words" in connection with the elements of infantile erotic play in language learning (p. 61). "Nothing but" is a dangerous phrase to apply to metaphor, which surely involves a very complicated kind of play, a species of play representing more than just pleasurable, primitive manipulation—the kind of complicated play that Brown's own later work so well displays, in fact. At one point Brown mentions tension in art: "It is the tension between the unconscious and the conscious which differentiates the play of the primary process in art from the play of the primary process in dreams" (p. 62). I believe it would make more sense to say that art incorporates secondary-process mentation far more than dreams do; that is, the stringencies imposed on art because of its appeal to the ego make for a greater degree of tension in art than in dreams, where sleep largely negates reality-testing. What differentiates the dream from art is not the way the primary process operates in each but the much greater role of secondary-process mentation in art and the way the two modalities function in concert.

In *Life Against Death* Brown speaks of language's infantile erotic base, of language as "essentially a neurotic compromise." But if language is a neurotic compromise "between the erotic (pleasure) and operational (reality) principles, it follows that the consciousness, in the artistic use of language, is subversive of its own instrument and seeks to pass beyond it" (p. 73). In *Love's Body* Brown calls for "speech resexualized." The call is for union at all levels and in all (polymorphous) ways—a cosmic fusion.

37. Norman O. Brown, *Life Against Death* (Middleton, Conn.: Wesleyan University Press, 1959), p. 55.

"The true meanings of words are bodily meanings, carnal knowledge; and the bodily meanings are the unspoken meanings."[38] This emphasis is invaluable because Brown alerts us to the intrinsic vitality of language, but it is misleading to the extent that the regressive features of his world view lead him to oversimplify some of the operations of the metaphoric process.

This oversimplification can be understood in the light of the "Boundary" chapter in *Love's Body*. Brown rejects Freud's argument in "The Two Principles of Mental Functioning" that with the acquisition of the reality principle one mode of thought activity becomes split off and kept free of reality-testing. Citing William Blake's contention that "Mental Things are alone Real," Brown adopts a monistic position at variance with Lockean and Cartesian notions of mental and nonmental reality. On this basis he argues that schizophrenics see the world more clearly than normal people. "Schizophrenics are suffering from the truth," says Brown. "It is not schizophrenia but normality that is split-minded; in schizophrenia the false boundaries are disintegrating." Brown assumes that schizophrenic thought approaches pure metaphor. Ironically, and contrary to common belief, schizophrenics do not use metaphor, at least not the way artists do. Schizophrenics use what is known as "unlabelled metaphor." Artists never lose sight of the difference, or boundary, between the literal and the figurative. For schizophrenics there is no difference. Whereas psychoanalysts view schizophrenics as trapped in private symbolic worlds they cannot distinguish from what we call reality, Brown regards schizophrenic thought as liberated from false boundaries between mental and physical categories. The monistic position Brown adopts, if I understand him correctly, makes it impossible for him to accept as significant a model treating reader response to poetry in terms of a tension-producing dynamic. There can be no homeostasis. For him, "Everything is only metaphor: there is only poetry."

With these considerations in mind, particularly such ideas as Coleridge's assumption that reading a poem should be an on-

38. Norman O. Brown, *Love's Body*, p. 265. See also Brown's further discussions of metaphor in *Closing Time* (New York: Random House, 1973) and "From Politics to Metapolitics," in *A Caterpillar Anthology*, ed. Clayton Eshleman (Garden City, N.J.: Anchor Books, 1971), pp. 7-20.

going pleasurable activity of a mind "excited by the attractions of the journey itself" and Ella Freeman Sharpe's assertions about body-oriented, revealing-and-concealing aspects of metaphor, I would like to present a reading of two lyrics by John Keats: the two sonnets on fame. My purpose is not so much to interpret the poems as to hypothesize about configurations of the reader's mentational responses to these poems. While these configurations will doubtless be overly schematized and unrealistically normative, I hope nevertheless to demonstrate the probability of certain kinds of response to certain places in the texts. Comparing these two poems, written in the same genre, on the same theme, at the same time (April 1819), by the same author, allows me to make inferences about the relationship between poetic quality and mentational intensity on the basis of assumed homeostatic differences in the reader's response to the imagery of the poems. Here are the sonnets, in the order they usually appear:

I

Fame, like a wayward Girl, will still be coy
    To those who woo her with too slavish knees,
But makes surrender to some thoughtless boy,
    And dotes the more upon a heart at ease;
She is a Gipsey, will not speak to those
    Who have not learnt to be content without her;
A Jilt, whose ear was never whisper'd close,
    Who thinks they scandal her who talk about her;
A very Gipsey is she, Nilus-born,
    Sister-in-law to jealous Potiphar;
Ye love-sick Bards! repay her scorn for scorn;
    Ye Artists lovelorn, madmen that ye are!
Make your best bow to her and bid adieu,
Then, if she likes it, she will follow you.

II

"You cannot eat your cake and have it too."—Proverb

How fever'd is the man, who cannot look
    Upon his mortal days with temperate blood,
Who vexes all the leaves of his life's book,
    And robs his fair name of its maidenhood;
It is as if the rose should pluck herself,
    Or the ripe plum finger its misty bloom,
As if a Naiad, like a meddling elf,
    Should darken her pure grot with muddy gloom;
But the rose leaves herself upon the briar,

> For winds to kiss and grateful bees to feed,
> And the ripe plum still wears its dim attire;
> The undisturbed lake has crystal space;
> Why then should man, teasing the world for grace,
> Spoil his salvation for a fierce miscreed?

Keats, who wrote to J. A. Hessey (8 October 1818) that he would "sooner fail than not be among the greatest," approaches the theme of fame in a playful manner in the first sonnet by giving us fame in the guise of a coquette. He expresses his ambivalence toward Fame by depicting her as something of a slut. She is desirable, yet deplorable. Worse, she is coy and can only be achieved by the stratagem of affecting scorn for her. Keats treats a subject apparently divorced from matters sexual, fame, in sexual terms in the first sonnet. In contrast, the second sonnet makes no direct comparison of fame to a woman, and, except for reference to the Naiad, to "fair name" as "maidenhood," and to the rose as feminine, it contains only one passage even remotely sexual: the winds kissing the rose. Instead of fame being like a woman, the man who seeks fame is himself like a woman in certain obscure ways. He will spoil or mar or dirty himself somehow if he strives too feverishly for fame. The two sonnets have quite similar "morals": (I) don't want too much or you'll be disappointed and (II) don't strive too hard or you'll mess things up.

Despite appearances, the second sonnet is far more steeped in sexuality than the first one, as attention to the way the two sonnets mobilize primary-process mentation will show. One fairly reliable indicator of the presence of primary-process mentation is the number of references to the body and its functions in any given passage. In the first sonnet there are only two or three direct ones: to "slavish knees," to the Jilt "whose ear was never whispered close," and possibly to "a heart at ease," though "heart" in this context is such a dead metaphor that its physiological aura is minimal. In the second sonnet there are five direct body references ("blood," "finger," "kiss," "feed," and "eat your cake," if we include the epigraph). More important than direct body references are the metaphors for body parts and functions ("maidenhood," "rose," "plum," the Naiad's "pure grot," and others). Most of the sexuality of the first sonnet is conscious; most of that in the second one unconscious. The first sonnet alludes repeatedly to conscious adult, heterosexual activity in such phrases as "way-ward Girl," "woo her," "makes surrender," "a Gipsey" (from a hot climate—"Nilus-born"), and the arousal value of these references depends very little on the vigor of the imagery, the major exception being the coital metaphor of line 7: the ear as a symbolic opening penetrable by symbolically sexual breath. One of the main sexual references, to the implied lust of Potiphar's wife's sister, relies on the reader's knowledge of the Bible, not on any symbolic value or synergistic force in the language of the line itself. For the most part the language of the second sonnet far exceeds that of the first in concreteness.

The first two quatrains compare man's feverish search for fame to a series of actions ranging from undesirable to unnatural ones. He cannot look with temperate blood upon his mortal days, he vexes the leaves of life's book, and he robs his name of its fair maidenhood—or purity, or virtue. Because of the synergistic way the image of blood in close conjunction with the metaphor of robbing maidenhood suggests a pun on "maidenhead," the reader will probably be cued to make unconscious genital associations with the subsequent imagery, a series of masturbation metaphors. The rose plucks herself, the plum fingers its misty bloom, and a Naiad darkens her pure grot with muddy gloom, a genital metaphor whose anal overtones compound the implied unnaturalness of the act. Since all of these metaphors express autoerotic activity, they are pregenital, a factor heightening the implied unnaturalness of the behavior in the context of the poem. An extraordinary degree of *interaction* energizes the metaphors of this quatrain, as can be seen in the sexual meaning of "meddling" (line 7). One meaning of "meddle," now obsolete, is "to have sexual intercourse." Shakespeare uses the word in this sense, and it derives from the Old French *medler,* the source for one of Shakespeare's favorite genital metaphors, "medlar." Even "elf" takes on the meaning, familiar in psychoanalysis, of the little man as symbolic phallus. A perfect psychosexual parallelism holds for "pluck," "finger," and "meddling elf," and for "rose," "plum," and "grot." Yet all of these metaphors remain meaningful expressions on the conscious level for unnatural acts. A rose ought not to pluck itself, and so forth. The conscious and unconscious levels of meaning simply reinforce each other, though in dynamic terms it might be more accurate to speak of how the feeling invested in the sexual metaphors invigorates the intellectual import of the lines.

The next four lines are antithetical to the earlier ones. The rose remains unplucked and leaves herself upon the briar. If her beauty is violated at all, it is only by natural forces: the kissing winds and feeding bees. She does not violate herself. The plum retains her dim attire—literally keeps her clothes on. In place of the Naiad's muddy grot we have the clarity, purity, and absence of turmoil of the undisturbed lake with crystal space. Just as the last four lines of the first sonnet provide a solution to the problem (the love-sick bards must cultivate scorn, or at least detachment), so the last six lines of the second sonnet offer an answer to the difficulties mentioned, only this answer is rather less easy to paraphrase than that of the first sonnet. Attempts to state the solution in some such terms as "Do not strive too hard" are legitimate, yet they do not account for the richness of the poem. Perhaps the proverb about eating your cake and having it, the epigraph, means in conjunction with the sonnet itself that the achievement of fame is impossible except at inordinate cost. Still, fame remains desirable, and the last six lines remain ambiguous to the point where no simple answer or solution is acceptable.

Experiencing the second sonnet to the fullest intellectual and emotional extent involves movement describable in terms of direction. There is an "up-down-up" movement from a relatively heavy participation in the secondary process in the first four lines, to an emphasis on the primary process in the next six lines, and back up to a high level of mentation in the last four lines. When the reader encounters metaphors like "mortal days," "temperate," the leaves of "life's book," and "fair name," his mind responds by operating in a relatively conscious, conceptual, "digital" way. It should be clear enough by now that the concrete metaphors of the middle of the poem precipitate considerable primary-process mentation; they are still "meaningful" in conscious terms but their main appeal is not at this level. A new upward movement commences in line 11. Beginning with the word "attire," which involves the secondary process more than a word like "clothes" would, the reader meets with a number of metaphors stimulating thought of a high conceptual order: the polysyllabic "undisturbed," "crystal space," "man" (for "mankind"), "world," "grace," "salvation," and "miscreed." That many of these words derive from religious and philosophical discourse contributes to the abstractness of the level of communication. This up-down-up psychostructural pattern is fairly common in literature.[39] It could also be described in other terminology, the characteristic movement being from reality to fantasy to reality, or from ego concerns to id concerns back to ego concerns, or from conscious to unconscious to conscious. Lewis Carroll's Alice, to give an extreme example, is conscious and bored as her sister reads a book; she falls asleep and into an underground wonderland, a bizarre world dominated by the primary process; and at the end of the book she awakes to the world of reality where she makes digital distinctions ("You're nothing but a pack of cards!") in preference to analogic associations.

The reader's experience of the second sonnet involves still another movement—a retrogressive one in the continuum of psychosexual development. From the adult genital activity of defloration in line four, the metaphors regress to autoerotic masturbation deriving from the phallic stage, and from there to an early oral stage of satisfaction, the only exception being in line 10 ("For winds to kiss and grateful bees to feed"), which has some genital overtones. Oral elements can be seen in the kissing winds, the feeding bees, the food value of the "ripe plum," and—if we include the epigraph—in eating cake. Correlating with the overall regressive movement of the poem is one from active to passive modes of behavior, a shift from active genital and phallic striving in metaphors having to do with penetrating the female body to the passive rose upon the briar, kissed by winds and fed upon by bees, the passiveness of the plum *wearing* its attire versus *fingering* its bloom, and the perfect inactivity of the undisturbed lake. This passivity contrasts sharply with the frenetic activity of the man in quest of fame who teases the world for grace—a fierce miscreed.

The second sonnet proffers the solution of an oral passivity to the problem of phallic striving. If so, what has this unconscious solution to do with fame, and—if there is a connection—how on earth did Keats come to treat such a subject in a libidinal frame-

39. This basic pattern was called to my attention by Norman N. Holland.

work? Though ostensibly divorced from sexuality, the desire for fame does have libidinal coordinates. This becomes apparent if fame be thought of in terms of narcissism, a form of self-love with erotic components. In the first sonnet the association of fame with a desirable woman is quick and easy, an act of fancy. In the second sonnet the idea of a man in search of fame being like a woman constitutes an act of the imagination. Strangely enough, Keats "abandons" this notion at the beginning of line 9. A new perspective takes its place that is different from, but closer to, the association of the first sonnet. If we think of the speaker as switching his identification at this point from the rose-plum-Naiad constellation to the kissing winds and feeding bees, then the feminine entities are transformed from subject-identifications to objects, to sources of gratification, as in the first sonnet, except that at the end of the second sonnet this source of gratification resembles the calm satisfactions of the mother's breast more than the lubricious charms of a no-longer-coy mistress. To be sure, the oral imagery is not specifically breast imagery, or maternal. Yet if my inferences are at all meaningful, the latter portion of the sonnet presents an idealized invisible mother who provides the ultimate source of personal peace and pure satisfaction with which the gratifications won by a worldly striving for fame can never quite compare, though man will seek them anyway.

According to the proposed model, the second sonnet generates far more psychic tension—experienced consciously, perhaps, as a relatively mild sensation of heightened sensibility and euphoric involvement—than the first sonnet will. A glance at the first sonnet shows how much inert verbiage it contains, as in lines 5-6: "She is a Gipsey, will not speak to those / Who have not learnt to be content without her." While these words do communicate something, they generate no conceptual thought of a high symbolic order and almost nothing in the way of primary-process mentation. The second sonnet works language for all it is worth. At the same time it mobilizes through sexual metaphor an enormous amount of primary-process mentation, it stimulates our minds to come to grips at a cognitive level with what it means to tease the world for grace and spoil our salvation for a fierce miscreed. In addition to the relative amount of emotion and thought it gives rise to, there is a radical difference in the range of mentation involved, cumulatively considered; that is, the second sonnet takes us down to deeper, more repressed levels of psychosexual concern than the genital sexuality of the first sonnet and forces us at the same time to experience a high range of symbolic meaning.

While it may be impossible with any exactitude to weigh the amount of primary process and secondary process in any given passage of poetry, the problem of estimating the quantity of each mode and its proportion to the other is nevertheless an important concern. Roy Schafer mentions the clinical problem corresponding to the critical task here at hand: "It is . . . a steady preoccupation of the psychoanalyst to assess the balance of the primary and secondary processes and shifting levels of organization in the patient," and in this connection he cites Loewald's emphasis on the analyst's need to experience a regression in the service of the ego if he is to comprehend what level the patient is communicating from.[40] Similarly, Harold Searles comments on the unceasing variation of level in schizophrenic communication, and adds, "There are even instances where the patient is functioning on more than one developmental level simultaneously."[41] As I have been stressing all along, this kind of multiple functioning is almost invariably the case with art. For the literary critic as well as the analyst, then, awareness of and participation in the mentational potential of the verbal texture he examines constitute an inevitable part of the analytic process. Since the value of Kris's concept of regression in the service of the ego has recently been challenged by Pinchas Noy,[42] it should be understood that my own reference to regression to the primary process has no pejorative implications whatsoever. On the contrary, such regression operating synergistically with higher ego functions is a vital aspect of the creative process and the responses it evokes.[43]

40. Roy Schafer, *Projective Testing and Psychoanalysis* (New York: International Universities Press, 1967), p. 110.

41. Harold F. Searles, *Collected Papers on Schizophrenia and Related Subjects* (New York: International Universities Press, 1965), p. 401.

42. Pinchas Noy, "A Revision of the Psychoanalytic Theory of the Primary Process," *Int. J. Psycho-Anal.* 50 (1969): 155-78.

43. I say "synergistically" because Noy's recent formulation of the role of the primary and secondary processes in art stresses their "integration," a metaphor tending to obscure the dynamic relationships involved. See Pinchas Noy, "A

To the extent that primary- and secondary-process modes of mentation can be located, and their proportions estimated, it becomes possible to approach the aesthetic problem of evaluating poetic language with some degree of objectivity, though it would be more accurate to speak of accounting for an evaluation *after the fact* since it cannot be demonstrated in any direct way that the sensed vitality or beauty of a passage of poetry for a given reader at a given time is proportional to the amount of tension generated. The demonstration must be indirect and has to be based on a variety of assumptions, including the premise that human beings can experience thought and feeling unconsciously, with only epiphenomenal ripples at the conscious surface of the mind.

A number of aesthetic questions remain. I might ask, to start with, if the second sonnet on fame has the attributes of beauty in any customary sense of the word. Some of the imagery could be called lovely in the conventional sense of metaphor as ornament: the crystal space of the placid lake, the ripe plum in its dim attire, the rose on the briar, kissed by winds and fed upon by bees. By similar standards, however, the earlier imagery of the rose plucking itself, the plum fingering its misty bloom, and the Naiad muddying her pure grot looks ugly. The trouble with honorific labels like "beautiful" is that they are so misleading in view of the unsavory elements so often lurking in literature. Lowes reminds us that "the primal stuff of poetry may be as utterly remote in nature from its metamorphosed state as the constituents of Helen's flesh and blood are unlike Helen's loveliness."[44]

One way of dodging the problem of evaluating poetry lies in believing the old adage that beauty is in the eyes of the beholder. I, for one, cannot accept the view that the experience of value in literature is entirely relative and purely subjective, regardless of what is in the poem. Neither can I accept Morse Peckham's contention that providing a powerful emotional response is not a function of art.[45] On the contrary, I think the intensity of our response to art has much to do with how we evaluate it—though

---

Theory of Art and Aesthetic Experience," *Psychoanalytic Rev.* 55 (1968): 636, 638, and 642.

44. *Road to Xanadu,* p. 74.

45. Morse Peckham, *Man's Rage for Chaos* (Philadelphia: Chilton Books, 1965), p. 219.

"response" in my terms has little to do with our conscious
response, emotional or intellectual. It seems likely that the *intensity* of our response to complex art will not be apparent because
of the emotional "balance" or "levelling" built into the homeostatic features of the response process.[46]

The problem might be reformulated in these borrowed words:
can we ever, like Euclid, gaze on Beauty bare? I fear not. Beauty
does not lie undraped on a couch of poetic images. "Beauty" is
simply one of a number of words we commonly use to account for
certain categories of subjective response to certain types of stim-
uli. In aesthetic theory, as Frederick Crews says, "one must decide
whether to see art as mental activity or as a direct apprehension
of truth and beauty."[47] While the former attitude is "less exalted
. . . it leaves the critic freer to trace the actual shape of a work
. . . including shifts of intensity and mood." I. A. Richards
lambasts the supposition that there is any such thing as a specifically aesthetic emotion and he defines value in art this way:
"Anything is valuable which will satisfy an appetency without
involving the frustration of some equal or more important appetency."[48] In psychoanalytic terms, the reader values literature
when it provides gratification without generating excessive anxiety. Norman Holland gives us this formula as part of his trans-
formational theory of literary experience: "We get the feeling
'this is good,' when a literary work successfully balances fantasy
and its handling of the fantasy, neither over-managing nor under-
managing it."[49]

To state the matter in terms of modal dynamics, the feeling
"this is good" will be strongest when poetic language stirs up a
great amount of the primary process in combination with enough
secondary-process mentation to keep the response process under
control—much as control rods in an atomic reactor govern the
generative process of nuclear fission. Thus the qualitative judgment of poetry depends, at least in part, on quantitative factors. A
qualitative term like "richness," applied in an honorific way to a

46. Cf. Miles D. Miller, "Music and Tension," *Psychoanalytic Rev.* 54 (1967):
141-56.
47. "Literature and Psychology," p. 81.
48. *Principles of Literary Criticism*, p. 48.
49. *Dynamics*, p. 312.

passage of poetry, cannot fail at the same time to register a quantitative perception. A word like "beauty" can imply quantity. If Helen of Troy was beautiful, then she had a lot of whatever it takes to provoke a certain kind of response.

Whether psychoanalysis listens with a third ear or looks with a third eye, it appears to be deaf and blind to beauty. Freud, not in the habit of philosophizing about the good, the true, and the beautiful, confesses in *Civilization and Its Discontents* that psychoanalysis has rather less to say about beauty than it does about most other things. But he does venture this statement about beauty: "All that seems certain is its derivation from the field of sexual feeling. The love of beauty seems a perfect example of an impulse inhibited in its aim."[50] Such qualities as attractiveness, he points out, are notable attributes of the secondary characteristics of the sexual object whereas "the genitals themselves, the sight of which is always exciting, are nevertheless hardly ever judged to be beautiful." By analogy, part of our awe of poetry may reflect what in Freud's language would be called an aim-inhibited sublimation of libido attaching itself to the poem rather than to what is in the poem.

50. Freud, *Std. Ed.* XXI, p. 83.

2

Modal Ambiguity

> Farewell sweet phrases, lovely metaphors.
> But will ye leave me thus? when ye before
> Of stews and brothels onely knew the doores,
> Then did I wash you with my tears, and more,
> Brought you to Church well drest and clad:
> My God must have my best, ev'n all I had.
> —George Herbert, "The Forerunners"

To consider language in relation to the primary and secondary processes requires considerable rethinking of the psychoanalytic theory of symbolism as it applies to words. Mark Kanzer observes in this connection that "to Caroline Spurgeon, a nose is a nose and, as an organ of smell, may indicate Shakespeare's preference for flowers and the aroma of good cooking; to Ernest Jones, it is uncompromisingly phallic."[1] Charles Rycroft tries to rectify this sort of one-sidedness on the part of psychoanalysis, epitomized in the essay to which Kanzer refers, Jones's 1916 paper called "The Theory of Symbolism," by arguing against the view that sexual symbolism belongs solely to the primary process and occurs only by virtue of repression. Rycroft assumes symbolization to be a general ability of the mind "which is based on perception and which may be used either by the primary or the

---

1. Mark Kanzer, "Imagery in *King Lear*," *American Imago* 22 (1965): 3.

secondary process."[2] I wish to call attention to Rycroft's tendency to speak of primary- and secondary-process symbolism in an either/or way, as though symbolism could occur in both systems but not simultaneously, as in this further instance: "Once a symbol has been formed it may be used either by the primary or the secondary process." David Beres uses similar phrasing: "The symbol once formed may serve either primary-process or secondary-process discharge."[3]

It is essential that symbolism be understood to function not in the one-sided fashion represented by Jones's tradition-bound view, nor even in the more comprehensive either/or way just mentioned, but in the most comprehensive way possible. According to my view, a literary symbol or a piece of symbolic behavior can and often will reflect both primary- and secondary-process functioning simultaneously. In fact Rycroft eventually rejects his earlier formulation when he realizes the fallacy of assuming a legitimate *conceptual dichotomy,* the primary and secondary processes, to be a universal discontinuity.[4] Elsewhere Beres also exhibits a more balanced, holistic view of symbolism than I have indicated, such as when he claims that "symbolism is an ubiquitous process present in all human activity."[5] My purpose in quoting unacceptable as well as acceptable remarks by Rycroft and Beres has been to emphasize the importance of keeping the idea firmly in mind that language can operate on more than one frequency at the same time. A century or so ago, for example, it was said that the three most beautiful words in the English language were "mother," "home," and "heaven." My point is that

2. Charles Rycroft, "Symbolism and Its Relationship to the Primary and Secondary Processes," *Int. J. Psycho-Anal.* 37 (1956): 137 and 144.

3. David Beres, "Symbol and Object," *Bulletin of the Menninger Clinic* 29 (1965): 20.

4. Personal communication, 10 June 1973. Dr. Rycroft made his rejection of the either-or view explicit and referred me to his later paper, "Beyond the Reality Principle," *Int. J. Psycho-Anal.* 43 (1962): 388-94. Though he specifies no particular passage, he presumably refers to such remarks as this one: "Under conditions of 'ideal' or 'normal' mental health these [two modes of mental functioning] are integrated and analysis of the totality of mental activity into discrete types of function is impossible" (p. 388). The papers mentioned above and other relevant observations can be found in Dr. Rycroft's important book, *Imagination and Reality* (New York: International Universities Press, 1968).

5. "Symbol and Object," p. 14.

the separate terms communicate ideas about beauty at a fairly abstract secondary-process level and *at the same time* they convey, as a group, a related yet quite different set of meanings constellated around the positive associations of rest, love, security, nurture, and so on, with maternal care.

In this chapter I will stress the coordinate operations of the primary and secondary processes characteristic of human response to complex language in such a fashion as to develop an hypothesis about the way ambiguity helps to generate synergistic patterns of thought and emotion.

A more elaborate example of such functioning than the mother-home-heaven triad can be discerned in a poem by George Herbert entitled "Vertue":

> Sweet day, so cool, so calm, so bright,
> The bridall of the earth and skie:
> The dew shall weep thy fall to night;
>   For thou must die.
>
> Sweet rose, whose hue angrie and brave
> Bids the rash gazer wipe his eye:
> Thy root is ever in its grave,
>   And thou must die.
>
> Sweet spring, full of sweet dayes and roses,
> A box where sweets compacted lie;
> My musick shows ye have your closes,
>   And all must die.
>
> Onely a sweet and vertuous soul,
> Like season'd timber, never gives;
> But though the whole world turn to coal,
>   Then chiefly lives.

What may be presumed to happen as a reader encounters the imagery of the second stanza, especially the metaphor of a rose so brilliant in hue as to seem angry, so striking as to bid the rash beholder to wipe his overstimulated eye? Within the theological context of the poem, the rose symbolizes natural beauty suffering organic decay and death during the course of a lifetime in contrast to the permanent beauty of a virtuous soul lasting through all eternity. At the same time this rare rose may possess another, complementary sort of meaning within the ambience of the primary process initiated by elements of the poem's first stanza, specifically the allusion there to the bridal and defloration of "sweet day." Because of the erotic overtones of the first stanza, the rose in the second stanza begins to accumulate primary-process resonance. As he responds to this metaphor the reader may form some "mental picture" of an actual rose—a dim, fleeting, synaesthetic one—in response to the complex verbal image of a sweet rose so vivid as to oblige the gazer to wipe his eye. The reader's mental image, if any, will probably be vaguely conscious and its "affective correlative" seemingly negligible in quantity while at the same time the poet's words will have triggered a considerable amount of unconscious primary-process mentation, genital in focus, whose only observable manifestation may be a sudden mental alertness, a kind of intellectual savoring of the imagery.

If the reader's response to the poem develops in stages during several readings, the unexpectedness of a color described as at once "angry"and "brave" may alert his natural secondary-process, problem-solving inclination to follow the poem's meaning and to understand specific transfers of meaning in given metaphors. This intellectual process may then give way to, or "float" on, unconscious primary-process associations of the rose with something more exciting than a flower. The two streams of mentation may then converge in the form of what could be called a hyper-cathected awareness of the beauty of the rose, the force of the poetry, and the metaphysical significance of the entire poem—all of this activity happening without any accession to consciousness of overtly sexual elements.

What I have characterized as a certain buoyancy in the primary-process response that partly supports the cognitive response at the surface corresponds to what Anton Ehrenzweig describes, with emphasis on visual perception, as a dedifferentiated, unconscious, free-scanning process.[6] A scanning process of this kind may be assumed to operate with an efficiency unmatched by the conscious intellectual eye. Unconscious or preconscious scanning can note rapidly and without effort a great many "cues" in the language of the poem. Besides recording the direct sexual implications of the *bridal* of sweet day as part of a

6. Anton Ehrenzweig, *The Hidden Order of Art* (Berkeley: University of California Press, 1971), esp. pp. 3-46.

larger configuration of a felicitous union (of earth and sky) in
nature, part of the primary-process scanning would attend to
other configurations of union, like sweet days and sweet roses
joined in sweet spring,

> A Box where sweets compacted lie.

It would be alert to pleasure configurations, as in the repeated use
of "sweet" and the several images of natural beauty, and this
scanning process might treat the visual trope of the rash gazer
wiping his eye as though it were a bold metaphor for penile
excitation dramatized in terms of visual overstimulation. Such a
response to this image would correlate with the possibility that
the root of the rose that dies in its grave belongs to the rose in
two senses, one of them a sense assuming a pun in the word "die"
on physical death and sexual orgasm, a frequent pun in the poetry
of Herbert's era.

I have deliberately chosen to talk about a poem that could be
said to have no sexual significance at all. I have done so for the
purpose of stressing two factors: possibility and ambiguity. Interpretation deals in possibilities, or probabilities, not in actualities
or certainties. Otherwise one might better speak of observation
than interpretation. Quite apart from whether someone interprets a text in the usual sense of sorting out meanings, experience
of a text depends on probability in terms of what the reader will
bring to the text and what configuration of possibility the writer
has imposed on his text, however inadvertently. This interpretation of "Vertue" stresses ambiguity by emphasizing that the
principal images of the poem may be regarded as merely sensuous (day, rose, and spring as nature metaphors) or both sensuous and sensual in reference (day, rose, and spring as involving
various joinings perceived as pleasurable, beautiful, and fleeting).
It seems to me that there is no way to rule out the *possibility* of
sensual elements in "Vertue." Certainly they cannot be ruled out
as incompatible with the religious fervor of Herbert's poetry. "I
know the projects of unbridled store," says Herbert in another
poem. "My stuffe is flesh, not brasse; my senses live." Nor can
sensual possibilities be ruled out as incompatible with Herbert's
metaphysical theme. On the contrary, they enhance it. To speak
just of the rose image, it symbolizes beauty and mutability at the

secondary-process level. At the primary-process level it represents the vulva, a source of pleasure different from but comparable to the pleasure we must experience in perceiving beauty. Simultaneously, the vulva represented by the rose represents in turn potential for the loss of something desirable corresponding to the mutability theme and contrasting with the eternal bliss to be enjoyed by the virtuous soul after that final conflagration of the flesh when the whole world turns to coal on Judgment Day.

To speak allegorically for a moment, it will be necessary at this point to pass through the mucky Slough of Obscenity as we draw nigh the Secret Places of the Muse on the otherwise, high, well-drained Road of Metapsychology. While no detour would enable us to arrive so easily and quickly at her abode, direct passage through a fair amount of filth will ensure safe arrival at a higher understanding of the power of poetic language as compared to that of obscene language.

Dirty words, as a class, have special properties setting them apart from ordinary diction. For one thing, they have extraordinary power to excite people—with disgust, anger, laughter, desire, and so forth, depending on the circumstances. Ferenczi speaks of this power when he notes that an obscene word compels the hearer "to imagine the object it denotes, the sexual organ or function, in substantial actuality."[7] Paradoxically, it would seem, those words leaving least to the imagaination nevertheless have the greatest appeal to it. Why? Does the power of obscene words lie in *what* they refer to, in the unmediated *directness* of the reference, or perhaps in the *vividness* (the "substantial actuality") of the imaginative pictures they compel? Strange to say, the forcefulness of dirty words may have comparatively little to do with any of these factors. With respect to reference, for example, Ferenczi notes that euphemistic allusions to sexual processes and technical designations of them produce no comparable effect— "at least not to the same extent as the words taken from the original, popular, erotic vocabulary of one's mother-tongue." There is, in short, a world of difference between words like "flatus" and "fart," though they share the same denotation and a

7. Sandor Ferenczi, "On Obscene Words," in *First Contributions to Psycho-Analysis* (London: Hogarth Press, 1952), p. 137.

similar directness of reference. As for the relative force of the
slang term in this case, crediting it with some kind of power to
compel imaginative activity does not explain the source of such
power.

One clue to what is after all no great mystery can be found in
Ferenczi's patient's reduced resistance to further analysis once he
was able to utter the word "fart." The force behind obscenity
must be roughly equivalent to the strength of repression in any
given case, a factor which can be put to use by the therapist
himself.[8] Another clue lies in Ferenczi's statement that obscene
words have the capacity of forcing the listener "to revive memory
pictures in a regressive and hallucinatory manner." This sounds
like a description of the primary process, though Ferenczi does
not use this concept in his essay. If this substitution be made, then
one measure of the verbal horsepower of obscene language is the
extent to which it generates primary-process mentation, whether
the products be completely unconscious or take the form of
involuntary hallucinatory images. By the same token, secondary-
process terminology of a semi-technical sort like "flatus" possesses defensive potential sufficient to inhibit the production of the
primary process under ordinary conditions.

The common ability of most obscenity and much poetry to
arouse the primary process can be examined for a moment in an
instance where obscenity and poetry appear to join forces. (The
following lines have been incorrectly attributed to Matthew Prior,
who probably would have been content to accept the attribution.)

On a Fart Let in the House of Commons

> Reader I was born, and cry'd,
> I crack'd, I smelt, and so I dy'd.
> Like Julius Caesar's was my Death,
> Who in the Senate lost his Breath
> Much alike entomb'd does lye
> The noble Romulus and I;
> And when I dy'd like Flora fair,
> I left the common Wealth my Heir.

A glance at this graffito reveals that its flagrant sexuality relates
to subject matter, not to diction. With the single exception of the

---

8. Marvin J. Feldman, "The Use of Obscene Words in the Therapeutic
Relationship," *American J. Psychoanalysis* 15 (1955): 45-58.

vulgar title, there is not one filthy word in the verse. Its immediate appeal is to the secondary process via conventional, calculated witticisms. Whether we consider this work to be a poem or relegate it to some lesser category of distinction, it will be apparent that like poetry, and unlike most obscenity, this work has enough ideational range to make significant demands on the reader's higher ego functions.

The three different sorts of diction mentioned can now be compared with respect to their appeal to the primary and secondary processes. For convenience these three classes of diction will be called "technical," "obscene," and "poetic." A verbal paradigm using the apocryphal Prior poem will be this series: "flatus"/ "fart"/ "die." A couplet from Dryden's "Mac Flecknoe,"

> About thy boat the little fishes throng
> As at the morning toast that floats along,

yields an anal triad with coprophagous complications: "feces"/ "shit"/ "morning toast." With reference to Herbert's "Vertue," a genital triad would be "vulva"/ "cunt"/ "rose." In order to secure a somewhat more substantial basis for comparison, two further examples will be added. One series can be generated with reference to a passage in Donne's elegy, "Loves Progress":

> Rich Nature hath in women wisely made
> Two purses, and their mouths aversely laid:
> They then, which to the lower tribute owe,
> That way which that Exchequer looks must go.

In this case the triad would be "vulva"/ "cunt"/ "purse," or "Exchequer." And finally, to shift from nouns back to a verb, we can consider what one psychoanalyst has called the principal obscene word in the English language.[9] A poetic analogue of this word can be found in the climactic passage of Marvell's "To His Coy Mistress":

> Let us roll all our strength, and all
> Our sweetness, up into one Ball:
> And tear our Pleasures with rough strife,
> Through the Iron gates of Life.

9. Leo Stone, "On the Principal Obscene Word of the English Language," *Int. J. Psycho-Anal.* 35 (1954): 30-56.

The series in this instance would be "copulate"/ "fuck"/ "tear our Pleasures . . . gates of Life."

A number of observations can be derived from correlating the examples tabulated here:

technical	obscene	poetic
flatus	fart	die
feces	shit	morning toast
vulva	cunt	rose
vulva	cunt	purse; Exchequer
copulate	fuck	tear our Pleasures . . . gates of life

The common basis within each horizontal series is denotation: however different in tone, connotation, and usage, the words and phrases within a given series refer essentially to the same entity or activity. The differences are more instructive. Almost no ambiguity whatsoever resides in the technical and obscene terms whereas the poetic words or phrases are invariably ambiguous. The word "die" refers to death of the body, flatus, and orgasm (as in "dy'd like Flora fair"), not to mention the complex anal ramifications (associations with money and cloacal birth) of related phrases like "left the common Wealth my Heir." Corresponding to the lack of ambiguity in the terms of a series is whether the terms are literal or figurative. While the technical and obscene words are obviously literal, the poetic words are always metaphorical. A further ambiguity of poetic language is that it is often both literal and figurative at the same time, as is true of "tear." In context it refers literally to hymenal rupture and figuratively to coital rapture, besides having the oral dimension of a ravenous haste harking back to the earlier lines about amorous birds of prey devouring Time (the *carpe diem* motif). From a topographical point of view the technical and obscene terms communicate almost exclusively at the level of consciousness whereas poetic language appeals to our minds consciously, preconsciously, and unconsciously. From a structural point of view the technical terms are ego-oriented, the obscene terms are id-oriented, and the poetic words offer a more balanced, coordinated appeal to id, ego, and superego.[10] In short, they operate accord-

10. Under certain conditions the dynamics of response to obscene words may be

ing to what is known in psychoanalysis as the principle of multiple function.[11] Most noticeable but perhaps least important are the differences of tone. Technical terms are essentially neutral and are designed to be. Obscene words are generally hot, strong, raw verbiage and are meant to be. Because they are so controlling and containing, the muted words of poetry usually appear mild in their surface effects.

The degree of power to affect the human mind possessed by each class of diction should be clear by this time. Technical terms are low-voltage. Obscene terms possess shock value, but their strong immediate impact has little cumulative energy, as in the boring experience I once had of listening to Norman Mailer say "shit" about fifty times during one lecture. In contrast, poetic metaphors generate a subtle interplay of forces in our minds that builds toward greatness in a quantitative way that has qualitative consequences, as in these lines by Gerard Manley Hopkins:

> The world is charged with the grandeur of God.
>   It will flame out, like shining from shook foil;
>   It gathers to a greatness, like the ooze of oil
> Crushed.

As a rule the potential power of the representative words within each series will vary according to the way they mobilize the primary and secondary processes. Technical words generally fail to mobilize the primary process, though they may tend to do so to a limited extent under some circumstances in some individuals, such as when young Stephen Dedalus becomes disturbed at seeing the word "foetus" carved in student desks of the anatomy theatre in *A Portrait of the Artist as a Young Man*. To the extent technical terms are literal, specific, and concrete in reference (though abstract in nature), they also fail to stir the higher, abstract conceptual reaches of the secondary process. Obscene words resemble technical words in failing to mobilize the upper conceptual realms, but unlike technical words and like poetic ones

---

more complex than I have indicated. As Mark Kanzer points out, "Without a superego to be overcome and shocked, the obscene word has no spice. Obscenity essentially assails the superego to the surprise and delight of the ego" (personal communication, 1971).

11. Robert Waelder, "The Principle of Multiple Function," *Psychoanalytic Quarterly* 5 (1936): 45–62.

they are so highly cathected as to generate primary-process mentation freely.

The reason why obscene words work so well in pornography is not simply a matter of superficial appropriateness. As they maximize primary-process mentation, they minimize the secondary-process mentation whose reality orientation is inimical to sloshing around in the sweet slush of fantasy. In the violent language of black oral poems known as "toasts," obscenity presumably generates primary-process mentation more charged with aggressive than sexual components, as in these beginning lines of one version of "Signifying Monkey":

There hadn't been no shift for quite a bit
so the Monkey thought he'd start some of his signifyin' shit.
It was one bright summer day
the Monkey told the Lion, "There's a big bad burly motherfucker
        [the Elephant] livin' down your way."
He said, "You know your mother that you love so dear?
Said anybody can have her for a ten-cent glass of beer."
He say, "You know your sister that's old and gray?"
Say, "He's the turd that caused her to be that way."
And the Lion knew that he didn't play the Dozens
and he knew the Elephant wasn't none of his cousins,
so he went out through the jungle with a mighty roar,
poppin' his tail like a forty-four,
knockin' giraffes to their knees
and knockin' coconuts from the trees.
He ran up on the Elephant under the coconut tree,
said, "Come on you big bad burly motherfucker, it's just you and me."[12]

Such language serves to contain and release tempestuous emotion in a controlled way by ritualizing it in comic narrative. Here is another example of comparable language use by an eight-year-old black boy, diagnosed as a "psychotic character," who was allowed to say anything he wished in the therapist's office: "One day he announced that he had the day before told his mother to her face that she was a 'mother-fucking shit-head asshole.' I wondered aloud about that, and he cheerfully admitted that he had not really said that to her. 'But,' in a conspiratorial voice, 'I could have called her something much worse.' 'Oh?' 'I could have called her a

12. In Bruce Jackson's *"Get Your Ass in the Water and Swim Like Me"*: *Narrative Poetry from Black Oral Tradition* (Cambridge, Mass.: Harvard University Press, 1974), p. 164.

nigger.'"[13] The languages of pornography and violence follow the line of least resistance in seeking power, though by tapping so directly into the primary process they sacrifice in ultimate force what they gain in the immediacy with which they arouse emotion.

Of the three types of diction specified, only poetic language has the potential for more or less simultaneously inducing both mentational modes to a significant degree. A phrase like "Iron gates of Life" in the context of Marvell's poem bestirs our minds to operate at a high, abstract, conceptual level and in the same instant of time (in Pound's phrase) it mobilizes preconscious vaginal imagery and unconscious associations linking "gates of Life" to the labial gates of birth. From a structural viewpoint, the language of Marvell's poem appeals to id and ego at the same time. A facet of this involvement can be found in the ego-oriented irony of the adjective "Iron" and the intellectually crucial theme of *carpe diem,* insisted upon by numerous references to one of man's most abstract concerns: time. As a love poem, "To His Coy Mistress" spans pleasure and pain, life and death, past, present, and future, transcending the incest taboo by condensing the vaginal gates of mother and mistress: the place begotten with the place to get.

I have been drawing attention to the power obscene words share with poetic metaphor by virtue of their capacity to foster primary-process mentation. At the same time it has been instructive to note that obscenity has little or no claim to what appears to be a fundamental characteristic of poetic language, ambiguity, also a characteristic of play, jokes, parapraxes, dreams, neurotic symptoms, and symbolism generally. That art tends to be ambiguous is well known. In literary criticism this basic assumption has led to endless analysis of the possible meanings of passages like "Beauty is truth, truth beauty . . ." but approaches to the problem have usually been confined to the bounds of conscious thought. Even William Empson says later in his career, after deciding "We had better stick to what the fool of a conscious mind is doing," that "something *quite* unconscious and unintentional, even if the

13. Lawrence Hartmann, "Some Uses of Dirty Words by Children," *J. American Academy of Clinical Psychology* (January, 1973): 112.

hearer catches it like an infection, is not part of an act of communication."[14] The gentleman who caught the clap will not agree. He will invoke the standard metaphor, "communicable disease," and swear he got more than he bargained for. But Empson is correct about one thing: "The machinations of ambiguity are among the very roots of poetry."[15]

Ernst Kris and Abraham Kaplan produced the classic psychoanalytic paper on the subject of aesthetic ambiguity.[16] The authors believe that for Empson ambiguity in literature has largely the status of an empirical finding, of something to be located in a work, something more or less decorative. They prefer to look upon ambiguity as a factor playing a central role in catalyzing a reaction to the poem in the mind of the reader. In other words, ambiguity does not function in poetry as a vehicle of content somehow poetic in itself but rather as an instrument through which a content becomes revitalized in the reader's mind (p. 258). After distinguishing certain kinds of verbal ambiguity, designated disjunctive, additive, conjunctive, integrative, and projective, Kris and Kaplan note that words, images, and fancies come to mind because of their emotional charge and that "the primary process exhibits to a striking degree the tendency to focus in a single symbol a multiplicity of references and thereby fulfils at once a number of emotional needs" (p. 254). Speaking of the primary process as "the well of inspiration" for the artist, they go on to make this dramatic claim: "The potential of a symbol contributes to a specifically aesthetic experience only if the interpretation of the symbol evokes the resources of the primary process" (p. 255).

Two explanatory metaphors dominate their account of aesthetic ambiguity: shifts in aesthetic *distance* and psychic *level*. Speaking of the artist's "purposive" and "controlled" regression of the ego, they maintain that the inspired creativity of the artist differs radically from an activity such as automatic writing under hypnosis. For the artist, they say,

14. William Empson, *Structure of Complex Words* (Ann Arbor: University of Michigan Press, 1967), p. 341.

15. *Seven Types of Ambiguity*, p. 3.

16. In Ernst Kris, *Psychoanalytic Explorations in Art* (New York: International Universities Press, 1952), pp. 243-64.

The process involves a continual interplay between creation and criticism, manifested in the painter's alternation of working on the canvas and stepping back to observe the effect. We may speak here of a *shift in psychic level,* consisting in the fluctuation of functional regression and control. When regression goes too far, the symbols become private, perhaps unintelligible even to the reflective self; when, at the other extreme, control is preponderant, the result is described as cold, mechanical, and uninspired. Poetry is, to be sure, related to trance and dream. . . . But it is also related to rigorous and controlled rationality. No account of the aesthetic process can be adequate without giving due weight to this "intellectual" component. [p. 254]

According to their analogy, the painter's physical *distance* from the canvas he works on corresponds to his *level* of psychic involvement at any given moment of the artistic process. A couple of pages later the authors speak of communication as involving "a sharing of *psychic level,*" and following this of "the psychic level of interpretation," where the metaphor applies directly to reader psychology. If the level of interpretation involves too little ego control, the inferred meanings are projective and lacking in integration whereas too much ego control gives an overintellectualized response lacking in pleasure (p. 256). A response will not be aesthetic, furthermore, "unless it also comprises a shift in *psychic distance,* that is, fluctuation in the degree of involvement in action" (p. 256).

At this point the authors cite the work of Edward Bullough, on whose concept of "psychical distance" they have drawn.[17] In the relevant paper Bullough distinguishes various kinds of distance, such as spatial and temporal, but concentrates on the more important concept of "psychical distance," which he defines as the distance between the self and the not-self, the not-self (or what he calls "the affections") being any sensations, perceptions, ideas, and so forth that may affect the self. He also defines artistic production as "the indirect formulation of a distanced mental context," thus corroborating Wordsworth's formula of "emotion recollected in tranquillity." And Bullough attends to various formal devices that create distance, like the pedestal in sculpture and the frame in painting. But Bullough muddles the concept of

17. Edward Bullough, "Psychical Distance," *British J. Psychology* 5 (1912): 87-118.

psychical distance in crucial ways. In spite of repeated comments about the value of aesthetic distance, he asserts that there is theoretically "no limit to the decrease of Distance" and that "both in appreciation and production, most desirable is the *utmost decrease* of Distance without its [complete] disappearance." This dubious statement contradicts the value he elsewhere places on psychical distance. It has the additional difficulty of being at odds with Bullough's recognition that sexual and other intimate body functions require what he calls "special precautions," that is, such matters need more, not less, distancing.

I dwell on Bullough's inconsistencies because they may underlie some of the confusion occasioned by the analogies of Kris and Kaplan. These analogies generally make good sense taken separately but do not jibe well with each other. Though they declare the art of poetry to be their subject, Kris and Kaplan do not explain poetry consistently in one set of terms (psychoanalytic); instead they resort to analogies from painting. Discussing shifts in psychic level, they say that when regression goes too far symbolism becomes private, which is not necessarily the case, whereas when control preponderates the resulting work is cold, mechanical, uninspired, which is not necessarily true either. Perhaps still another analogy will show why. For the "artist" on a high-wire in a circus, the greater the danger, analogous to involvement, the greater the need for control. This combination of deep involvement with high control offers the greatest satisfaction for the identifying, empathizing audience. In poetry, similarly, deep regression is not necessarily separate from but may occur alongside or accompanied by a high degree of ego control (distance, detachment). Expressed in modal terms, poetry may exhibit a high degree of primary- and secondary-process mentation more or less simultaneously. Here is the difference between sheer fantasy—as in dreams—and art: dreams are almost pure primary process whereas art is characterized by a combination of primary and secondary process. Good metaphor epitomizes this combination.

Kris and Kaplan discuss very little poetry. They confine their attention to ambiguity at the conscious level when they do examine poetry. Almost everything they say about the various kinds of ambiguity they enumerate fails to show the primary process in action. And they usually speak of verbal ambiguity in terms of "meanings," "communication," and "interpretation," all of which suggest conscious response. But of course these are only minor flaws in a paper that can be said to provide the foundations of a psychoanalytic approach to the language of poetry. As for terminology, what follows will ignore the metaphors of distance and level used by Kris and Kaplan, retain their emphasis on the way ambiguity promotes—and is promoted by—the polysemous character of the primary process, and try to promote understanding of the dynamics of language by introducing still another category of ambiguity.

The trouble with the word "ambiguity" is that it is not ambiguous enough. Standard usage tends to limit its denotational range to multiplicity of meaning within the realm of conscious thought or ideation, though nothing in its root meaning of "lead, drive, wander about" would appear to impose such a limitation. Psychoanalysis generally uses another, not quite comparable, term to signify multiple feeling, namely "ambivalence." In practice this refers to more or less contrary affects experienced simultaneously. A comprehensive term is needed for expressing two broad kinds of meaning: ideational and emotional. Instead of coining a new word, I will employ the term "ambiguity" to characterize language which broadly speaking may be said to refer to conscious or unconscious thoughts or emotions. With this distinction in mind, I will define the concept of *modal ambiguity* as a characteristic of any ambiguous structure—such as a word, phrase, or poem—reflecting or appealing to one or both of the two mentational modes: the primary and secondary processes.

So defined, modal ambiguity might appear to be ubiquitous in human affairs. In theory, perhaps it is. In practice, it is not. While an absolutely unambiguous statement may be as difficult to generate as a random number, most statements in everyday discourse, like "Please hand me the coathanger," do not under normal circumstances contain or mobilize any ambiguity of primary- or secondary-process mentation. As a practical matter, then, useful distinctions can be made about the presence and degree of modal ambiguity in verbal structures.

Essentially simple yet completely flexible, the concept of modal ambiguity contains or is consonant with all combinations of multiple meaning describable in terms of any of the following referential coordinates: ideational, emotional; lexical, contextual; developmental (oral, anal, phallic, oedipal, genital); topographical (conscious, preconscious, unconscious); structural (id, ego, superego); and informational (analog, digital). Modal ambiguity covers all the ground referred to by the principal types of ambiguity named by Kris and Kaplan (disjunctive, additive, conjunctive, integrative, and expressive), though it does not of course amount to a substitute for these terms, which have their own particular descriptive value. To consider just one of these terms by way of illustrating how modal ambiguity covers similar ground, Kris and Kaplan suggest that ambiguity becomes "expressive" when its interpretation involves shifts of psychic level and distance. Since both "distance" and "level" appear to be topographical concepts, the idea of modal ambiguity comprehends that of expressive ambiguity, and it would follow that the greater the amount of modal ambiguity in a verbal entity, the more expressive it would be in the sense Kris and Kaplan use this term. The seven types of ambiguity enumerated by Empson also easily fall within the scope of the concept of modal ambiguity.

This concept can be subdivided into *intermodal* and *intramodal* ambiguity. A metaphor, image, word, or phrase having coordinates in both primary- and secondary-process mentation can be said to possess *inter*modal ambiguity. A metaphor, image, word, or phrase having more than one referent within either the primary process or the secondary process has *intra*modal ambiguity. Both types of ambiguity can, and sometimes do, reside in a single word or image (in a larger verbal context). Thus great complexity of thought and feeling can reverberate within the well-wrought urn of a single metaphor, as we may see by reconsidering the dug image in Cleopatra's suicide speech. The word "dug" contains the simple, lexical meaning of "nipple"; the larger lexical meaning of "breast"; the still larger secondary-process contextual meanings of "breast that feeds," "breast that feeds each alike, regardless of station, be he beggar or Caesar," and the more attenuated, affect-tinged ideas of "breast that gives satisfaction" and "breast that leads to sleep or sleep-like death." All of these more or less conscious meanings culminate roughly in the idea of the dug of death or the idea of death as something attractive, especially in that the sleep (death) leading us to this dug "never palates more" the dug of life—the meaning of all this being that the dug of death is especially attractive because it is perceived, in contrast to the precariousness of fortune, as a completely permanent, dependable source of satisfaction. Interweaved with our secondary-process response to these meanings in Shakespeare's passage— separable only by retrospective analysis but not as the responses occur—are the overlapping primary-process responses to the dug image. This image, a highly cathected one, expresses such feelings as "the breast is good," "I want the breast," and the related wishes of "I want food, security, status, fame, and surcease of all painful excitation, including loss of love objects"—a set of wishes spilling over into affectively negative attitudes toward both life and death, including fear of death, surfeit at the capricious breast of life, and weariness. This ambivalence accounts for the presence of this particular word rather than the more expected, more positive word "breast." In sum, the dug image gives us the special riches of both types of modal ambiguity—an instantaneous feast of thought and feeling without any mental indigestion resulting from so rapid an intake.

Metaphor is a natural vehicle of modal ambiguity. That Aristotle understood as much can be inferred from his remarks in the *Rhetoric* on the complex nature of artistic metaphor. He suggests that good metaphor will be lucid, pleasing, not farfetched, appropriate, yet "strange" (as opposed to familiar) and very much like a riddle (Bk. III, chap. 2), an odd combination of requirements but one which the dug metaphor appears to fulfil. What Aristotle calls the riddling aspect of metaphor seems less mysterious in light of a recent suggestion that metaphors provide an effective method for "tracking down" the main elements of a repressed idea because they so well serve the double function "of conveying the meaning of an intentional train of thought and, simultaneously, that of a repressed train of thought."[18] The ridling aspect of metaphor also corresponds to Freud's observation

18. George S. Klein, "Peremptory Ideation: Structure and Force in Motivated Ideas," in *Motives and Thought: Psychoanalytic Essays in Honor of David Rapaport,* ed. Robert R. Holt, (New York: International Universities Press, 1967), p. 120.

in the Dora case that ambiguous words can act as "switch-words" resembling a junction on a railway where cars can be switched to another set of rails.[19] Thus ambiguity in metaphor facilitates switching a "train of thought" back and forth from conscious to unconscious levels, or from neutral to cathected material. The more ambiguity generated by the metaphors of a poem, the more switching the reader will encounter and the greater the potential for the resultant mental oscillations to reinforce or amplify each other.

This remark implies mutuality between emotional power and ideational reference, yet the relationship of the two factors is by no means altogether clear. If anything, one might expect that power would align itself with lack of ambiguity, as in the case of obscene language, or that power might somehow be dissipated through the vibration of too many referential nodes. At the same time it seems as though power in poetry must result from some kind of combination or reinforcement of lesser units; otherwise the manifold thoughts and feelings apparent in Cleopatra's soliloquy might cancel each other out. What is the metapsychology of the amplification process? How can what one analyst refers to as the issue of ideational intensity and the problem of "the motivational intensity of a repressed train of thought" be accounted for?[20]

It seems to me that the concept of condensation accounts more than any other in psychoanalysis for the synthesizing power of the primary process, especially since it describes a mechanism possessing the extraordinary ability to combine not only thought with thought and emotion with emotion, but thought with emotion as well. At first glance this might appear a facile assumption because common usage of the term "condensation" does not always include dynamic implications. Even Freud's explanation, in places, ignores energy factors. In the *Introductory Lectures*

19. Freud, "Fragment of an Analysis of a Case of Hysteria," *Std. Ed.* VII, p. 65.
20. Klein, "Peremptory Ideation," p. 80. Until the current trend away from energy concepts toward ideomotor, informational models of mentation comes to fruition, if it does, we will have to continue to rely on energy concepts, as I do to a considerable extent in this book while knowing full well the theoretical difficulties inherent in the concept of psychic energy. As B. Rubinstein admits (in Holt's *Motives and Thought*, p. 73; see note 18), before we can eliminate the term "psychic energy" we will have to find a better process term to replace it with.

(1916-1917) he says that as a result of condensation the manifest level of the dream is "less rich" than the latent level, explaining that condensation is accomplished in three ways: (1) by complete omission of some latent thoughts; (2) by the omission of parts of some latent thoughts; and (3) by the combining of two or more latent thoughts with similar characteristics; a verbal example would be the *famillionär* jest in the book on jokes.[21] But all these combinations appear to be ideationally referential rather than energic, as is also true of the discussion of "switch-words" in the Dora case. In chapter VII of *The Interpretation of Dreams*, however, Freud speaks of the way the dream-work makes use of "displacement of psychical intensities," and in what amounts to a description of certain aspects of the primary process he mentions the possibility of the intensities of some ideas being discharged on, or transferred to, other ideas. "Since this process is repeated several times, the intensity of a whole train of thought may eventually be concentrated in a single ideational element."[22] An example of this process of concentration can be found in the large number of highly cathected associations which come into focus in the rat phobia in Freud's "Notes Upon a Case of Obsessional Neurosis" (1909), where rats (*Ratten*) are associated with torture, a childhood case of worms, anal eroticism, a gambler (*Spielratte*), advice (*Rat*), installments (*Raten*), children, the phallus, and marriage (*heiraten*), among other things. To return to *The Interpretation of Dreams*, in the course of one long paragraph Freud veers away from energy concepts like "discharge" to explanation in terms of signification, as in the phrase "*intensification of its ideational content*" (p. 595). That the concept of condensation does include the idea of concentration of psychic energy finds expression in this definitive statement on the nature of mentational dynamics: "The cathectic intensities [in the *Ucs.*] are much more mobile. By the process of *displacement* one idea may surrender to another its whole quota of cathexis of several other ideas. I have proposed to regard these two processes as distinguishing marks of the so-called *primary psychical process.*"[23]

It follows that the potential resources at the beck and call of the

21. Freud, *Jokes and Their Relation to the Unconscious, Std. Ed.* VIII, p. 18.
22. *Std. Ed.,* V, p. 507.
23. "The Unconscious," *Std. Ed.,* XIV, p. 186.

poet able to undergo regression in the service of the ego are simply enormous. He has available to him a mentational mode capable of combining both ideational multiplicity and the total psychic intensity with which the various ideas may be cathected. This mode of mentation possesses the tremendous speed and flexibility of an electronic computer because the mobility of cathexis operates through the virtually frictionless mechanisms of condensation, displacement, and plastic representation, not to mention the flexibility resulting from the exemption of primary-process elements from mutual contradiction—its freedom from the strictures of the reality principle and the plodding arduousness of methodical cognitive processes.[24] These possibilities for developing ambiguity, when combined with the degree of ambiguity also possible within the range of full consciousness, make poetic language a substance as malleable as "gold to airy thinness beat"—and more precious.

A blasphemous little poem by William Butler Yeats provides a text suitable for illustrating the range and flexibility of modal ambiguity in literature. The brevity of this verse lends itself to demonstrating condensation, and the perfection of its vulgarity fits well with the earlier discussion of poetry and obscenity. Here is the poem, a slender exercise in the delicate art of ultimate derogation:

> A Stick of Incense
>
> Whence did all that fury come?
> From empty tomb or Virgin womb?
> Saint Joseph thought the world would melt
> But liked the way his finger smelt.

The first two lines are reminiscent in their epic scope of Yeats's portrayal of the conception of Helen and Clytemnestra in "Leda and the Swan":

> A shudder in the loins engenders there
> The broken wall, the burning roof and tower
> And Agamemnon dead.

With something like the same degree of awe one could find in the spectacle of the conflagration of Troy, except that it is not awe

24. Ibid., p. 187.

but a mockery of awe detailed in mock-heroic fashion, Yeats asks in "A Stick of Incense" how the enormity that was Christianity could have issued from a virgin womb (the Virgin Birth) or an empty tomb (the Resurrection). The last two lines of the poem destroy the miraculous or mythic perimeters of Christianity—though not the historical ones implied by "all that fury"—by their reduction of the grand dogma of the Immaculate Conception to the coital realism of "thought the world would melt" and the olfactory realism of "liked the way his finger smelt." One ambiguity in the last two lines is that Yeats promotes Saint Joseph to the status of actual father at the same time he ridicules him (and Christianity by extension) by means of the digital metaphor. The understatement of "liked" in the final line is so incongruous with the cosmic image of "world would melt" as to make Saint Joseph appear fatuous. The force of the second line of the poem lies in the way it mocks the possibility of a virgin womb being any more fruitful than an empty tomb through a clever apposition of psychosexually similar metaphors, the associations involved being reinforced by the line's internal rhyme about an internal space.

Several lines of derision come together in the title of the poem. The rich ambiguity of "stick of incense" allows for the possibility of these references. It can denote an elongated piece of incense. Because of the associational link between the odor of incense and Saint Joseph's smelly finger, the title—and hence the entire poem—becomes a metaphor for a metaphor for a metaphor, that is, Saint Joseph's finger represents his penis, so the stick of the title becomes a metaphor for the finger—and by extrapolation a metaphor for the genesis of Christianity. There cannot be a virginal mother or a miraculous Christianity any more than fingers can make babies. If we consider as well that incense is associated with worship, and read the title as ironic, then the entire poem becomes a phallically aggressive repudiation of Christianity. But "incense" has still another sense if we call to mind the anal-erotic features of the myth of the Annunciation as Ernest Jones explains them in "The Madonna's Conception through the Ear."[25] While Yeats does not refer to the myth of aural concep-

25. Ernest Jones, *Essays in Applied Psycho-Analysis* (New York: International Universities Press, 1964), II, pp. 266-357.

tion, the importance of odors in the poem suggests that Yeats managed unconsciously to tune in to the magical equivalence of breath, flatus, penis, and semen in the myth. If this be so, then the stick of the title is a smelly one indeed: a stick of incense as a metaphor for a stick of smell as a metaphor for a penis. One begins to lose track of what represents what: a stick-like title standing for a stick-like poem resembling a stick-like finger with which an incensed imagination points in mockery at the supposed miraculous origins of Christianity.

Perhaps this version of the myth serves metaphorically as a kind of screen memory, wrought into poetry, of the poet's (and reader's) retrojection of his own conception. Should this be true, then the demythologizing of the marvel of the Immaculate Conception contains the sublimated seeds of the artist's demythologizing of the awful primal act of his own parents. The poet as creator recreates his own creation. In this connection the word "melt" provides a choice instance of intramodal ambiguity. "Melt" combines a genital metaphor for orgasm with an oral metaphor for fusion. As Freud phrases it, the boundary between ego and object at the coital climax threatens "to melt away."[26]

At the level of the secondary process Yeats's laconic iconography makes strong cognitive demands upon us by its theological references to the Christian dogmas of the Immaculate Conception, the Virgin Birth, the Resurrection, and indirectly to the theological intricacies of Saint Joseph's husbandly but nonbiological role and to the mystery of the divine potency of the Holy Ghost. Another side of the secondary-process appeal of the poem lies in its wit. A considerable amount of the erotic material in the poem is transparently intentional. To the extent Yeats handles this material with deliberate wit the reader encounters an appeal to higher mental functions. Add to these factors Yeats's artistic control over the formal aspects of the poem, which will be experienced on the part of the reader as a reassuring sense of ego mastery over affectively dangerous material, and I think it can be seen how much ambiguity, both intermodal and intramodal, this poem contains.

Pound's definitions of an image as "an intellectual and emotional complex in an instant of time" and "a vortex or cluster of fused

26. *Std. Ed.*, XXI, p. 66.

ideas . . . endowed with energy," cannot be improved, but they can be rephrased for illustrative purposes in light of the foregoing remarks. Some such wording as this might do: Poetic imagery, at its most creative moments, mobilizes simultaneously a maximum amount of primary-process mentation and an optimum amount of coordinate secondary-process mentation, thereby generating a cluster of ideas in a vortex of emotional energy. To the extent that such a formulation is grounded in reasonably precise and sufficiently complex assumptions concerning the basic modalities of the mind experiencing the poetic imagery, it conceptualizes the operations of poetic language in a manner accounting for the speed of the poetic process, for its emotional intensity, for its referential succinctness—and for the strange way in which the poet's "seething brains" and "shaping fantasies" apprehend "more than cool reason ever comprehends."

The Flesh Made Word

3

The Flesh Made Word

~~~~~~

> Not merely is the Heart a Hornbook, It is the Minds
> Bible, it is the Minds experience, it is the teat from
> which the Mind or intelligence sucks its identity.
> —Keats

> The ego is first and foremost a bodily ego.
> —Freud

Hawthorne neglects to specify precisely what he means by "the
humblest medium of familiar words and images" except to differ-
entiate this kind of language from the learned discourse of
Dimmesdale's fellow ministers. The terms "humblest" and "familiar" suggest Hawthorne may have had in the back of his mind
Wordsworth's advice to poets to use commonplace diction, the language of real men. Just exactly what the sources of the diction of the
common man might be is a question Wordsworth evades. Coleridge announces his intention at the beginning of *Biographia
Literaria* to effect a settlement of the poetic-diction controversy.
He manages to refute Wordsworth concerning the alleged lack of
difference between the language of prose and poetry but leaves us
in the dark about the appropriate sources of imagery.

  Is the language of poetry a special one? If so, how? Aristotle
recommends that metaphors should be derived from beautiful
words, the old idea of language as ornament, and he gives "rosy-

fingered dawn" as an instance (*Rhetoric*, 1405b). For much better advice I would like to turn to a series of examples Aristotle gives elsewhere. I have italicized the images of particular interest, though Aristotle has nothing more in mind at this point than emphasizing the basic similarity of metaphor and simile. He says Pericles compares the Samians with children "who *weep* while they accept *tidbits*." Demosthenes likens the people to "*seasick* passengers on a ship. Democrates compared politicians to nurses who *gulp down the morsels of food* themselves and *rub the baby's lips with their spittle*. Antisthenes said that Cephisodotus, who was very *thin*, was like incense: both delighted people by disappearing" (*Rhetoric* 1407a). In this clump of apparently disparate examples of effective simile a surprising number of references to the human body and its functions occur. It could be a coincidence, but I suggest the pattern has significance. These examples, including "rosy-fingered dawn," point to exactly what psychoanalytic theory would lead us to expect: that in his own body the poet finds a rich mine of metaphorical ore.

In this chapter I will try to detail what I have already called attention to in passing: the vitality contributed to poetry by the presence of significant body imagery. The reason why, as I have said, is that such body imagery tends to stimulate primary-process mentation in the reader and thereby engender the complex cognitive and emotional turmoil characteristic of a creative response to the poem on the part of the reader. Two important factors involved are the incidence of body imagery—the sheer amount of it tending to aggregate, if not multiply, the effect of the images in the reader's mind—and the degree of modal ambiguity, or complexity of reference, of the images, both in isolation and in concert. In addition, body imagery probably promotes functional regression in the reader's mentation. Only when his primary-process capacity has been fully activated can the reader benefit from its complex, multiple-track, incredibly efficient scanning and synthesizing potentialities.

Looking for body imagery in poetry strikes me as an enterprise resembling those occasions when an important gestalt remains virtually invisible in its ground until one actually starts seeking it out in a deliberate way, at which point one's sudden shift in perceptual focus makes altogether obvious what was not even apparent only a moment earlier. At the risk, then, of appearing to belabor what may soon seem obvious, I will try to effect such a shift in perceptual focus.

Consider, to begin with, the incidence of body imagery in one of the setpieces of literature, a passage so famous that every grammar-school teacher would stuff it down the gullets of his pupils, that they might then regurgitate Poetry. It is Jacques' speech on the seven ages of man:

> At first the infant,
> Mewling and puking in the nurse's arms.
> Then the whining schoolboy, with his satchel
> And shining morning face, creeping like snail
> Unwillingly to school.

Then we have the lover, "sighing like furnace," making a woeful ballad "to his mistress' eyebrow." After the soldier, bearded like the leopard, Shakespeare gives us a justice "in fair round belly with good capon lined," his eyes severe and beard of formal cut.

> The sixth age shifts
> Into the lean and slippered Pantaloon
> With spectacles on nose and pouch on side,
> His youthful hose, well saved, a world too wide
> For his shrunk shank, and his big manly voice,
> Turning again toward childish treble, pipes
> And whistles in his sound. Last scene of all,
> That ends this strange eventful history,
> Is second childishness and mere oblivion,
> Sans teeth, sans eyes, sans taste, sans everything.

That the corporal content of this speech is not so much exceptional as typical becomes more clear when we consider Shakespeare's most powerful single poem, *King Lear,* in which the basic recurrent metaphor, says Caroline Spurgeon, is that of "a human body in anguished movement, tugged, wrenched, beaten, pierced, stung, scourged, dislocated, flayed, gashed, scalded, tortured and finally broken on the rack."[1] It is of some moment, then, that Spurgeon claims the proportion of body images in Shakespeare far exceeds that of any other dramatist she examines (Marlowe,

---

1. Caroline F. E. Spurgeon, *Shakespeare's Imagery* (Cambridge at the University Press, 1966), p. 339.

Jonson, Chapman, Dekker, and Massinger), though she herself attaches no special importance to this difference other than its being a distinguishable feature (p. 49).

In an appendix she offers a "detailed" account of the subject matter of imagery in two plays. The images of one, *Romeo and Juliet,* she breaks down into such categories as nature, personification, animals, fire and light, food and cooking, war and weapons, sickness and medicine, sport and games, and so on. Under "Body and Bodily Action" she lists a grand total of five images for the entire play, four of bodily action and one reference to parts of the body. The reader skeptical enough of such an accounting to check the text for himself will encounter an avalanche of some forty-six references to the human body and its activities in the first sixty lines of the first scene! These begin with a number of metaphors on the theme of courage: body movements of striking, stirring, standing, moving, and running. They then spill over into the epitome of a phallocentric conception of courage when the clownish Sampson speaks of women, the weaker "vessels," being ever "thrust" to the wall and then brags, "Therefore I will push Montague's men from the wall and thrust his maids to the wall." Sampson says he will show himself a tyrant.

> Sam. When I have fought with the men, I will be cruel with the maids. I will cut off their heads.
> Gre. The heads of the maids?
> Sam. Aye, the heads of the maids, or their maidenheads—take it in what sense thou wilt.
> Gre. They must take it in sense that feel it.
> Sam. Me they shall feel while I am able to stand. And 'tis known I am a pretty piece of flesh.
> Gre. 'Tis well thou art not fish. If thou hadst, thou hadst been poor John [dried salted hake]. Draw thy tool. Here comes two of the house of Montagues. [Enter Abraham and Balthasar]
> Sam. My naked weapon is out. Quarrel—I will back thee.

This foolishness soon degenerates into the language of dumb show (or thumb show):

> Gre. I will frown as I pass by, and let them take it as they list.
> Sam. Nay, as they dare. I will bite my thumb at them, which is a disgrace to them, if they bear it.
> Abr. Do you bite your thumb at us, sir?
> Sam. I do bite my thumb, sir.

Were the proportion of body images to continue at this rate, this play of nearly three thousand lines would contain not five body images but over twenty-two hundred!

There is no need to number petals on a rose. I simply wish to stress how much body imagery Spurgeon overlooks because the sheer amount of it, though not the exact amount, affects the reader's response to this play and to poetry in general. Nor are these passages plucked out of context. A phallic viewpoint relevant to the deepest psychological themes of the play pervades the text. One sees comic versions of this theme in Mercutio's way of expressing the time of day: "The bawdy hand of the dial is now upon the prick of noon," to which the Nurse responds, "Out upon you! What a man you are!" One sees a tragic version of this phallicism in the swordsmanship of Tybalt and Romeo, and a culmination of the theme of a phallic unripeness when Juliet snatches Romeo's dagger and thrusts it in her body:

> O happy dagger!
> This is thy sheath. [Stabs herself] There rust, and
> let me die.
>   [5.3.169]

The tragedy is full of all kinds of body imagery. Here are Romeo's eloquent first words to Juliet:

> If I profane with my unworthiest hand
> This holy shrine, the gentle fine is this,
> My lips, two blushing pilgrims, ready stand
> To smooth that rough touch with a tender kiss.

And here is the soft witchery of Juliet's response:

> Good pilgrim, you do wrong your hand too much
> Which mannerly devotion shows in this;
> For saints have hands that pilgrims' hands do touch,
> And palm to palm is holy palmer's kiss.

Mercutio's speech about Queen Mab, who is no bigger than an agate stone on the *forefinger* of an alderman, bursts with references to the body. Toward the close of the play Romeo cries that Death has sucked the honey of Juliet's breath, and a few lines later he declares,

> Oh, here
> Will I set up my everlasting rest,
> And shake the yoke of inauspicious stars
> From this world-wearied flesh. Eyes, look your last!
> Arms, take your last embrace! And lips, O you
> The doors of breath, seal with a righteous kiss
> A dateless bargain to engrossing death!

Bodily awareness so saturates the play that we even learn—shortly before the Nurse mentions putting wormwood on her dug to wean Juliet—how many teeth she has left in her head: four, to be exact. Nor are these particular plays isolated instances, though imagery varies from work to work. For trial, the reader may thumb at random in Shakespeare to see how many times he can chance upon a dozen consecutive lines without at least one image pertaining to the human body (broadly construed to include any portion of the body; food, clothing, shelter; disease; physical movement; physiological processes; and the like).

In *Sartor Resartus,* a work superabundantly imbued with body consciousness, we are told that though in most speculations man has figured, tacitly, as a clothed animal, he is by nature a "Naked Animal." Lives there a man who can imagine a naked Duke of Windlestraw addressing a naked House of Lords? we are asked. We are assured that only to the eye of vulgar logic can the answer to "What is man?" be "an omnivorous Biped that wears Breeches." When Carlyle turns his attention to the nature of imaginative language, he perceives it in corporal terms:

> Language is called the Garment of Thought: however, it should rather be, Language is the Flesh-Garment, the Body, of Thought. I said imagination wove this Flesh-Garment; and does not she? Metaphors are her stuff: examine Language; what, if you except some few primitive elements (of natural sound), what is it all but Metaphors, recognised as such, or no longer recognised; still fluid and florid, or now solid-grown and colourless? If those same primitive elements are the osseous fixtures in the Flesh-Garment, Language,—then are Metaphors its muscles and tissues and living integuments. An unmetaphorical style you shall in vain seek for: is not your very *Attention a Stretching-to?*[2]

The discourse then touches on various kinds of literary style and mentions the problem of "sham Metaphors, which overhanging

2. Thomas Carlyle, *Sartor Resartus* (New York: Odyssey Press, 1937), p. 73.

that same Thought's-Body (best naked), and deceptively bedizen-
ing, or bolstering it out, may be called its false stuffings, superfluous
show-cloaks (*Putz-Mäntel*), and tawdry woollen rags: whereof he
that runs and reads may gather whole hampers—and burn them."

Carlyle's comparisons are more than idle, decorative transfers
condemning decoration. They help to point up how little attention literary criticism has paid to the corporeality of literary
language. Kenneth Burke proves an exception. Impacted in an
essay called "The Thinking of the Body," which offers comments
on catharsis imagery in literature so various as *Alice in Wonderland, Prometheus Bound,* and the poetry of Mallarmé, lies a little
joke about Burke's "labyrinthine task of trying to solve the Riddle
of the Sphincter." And in "Somnia ad Urinandum: More
Thoughts on Motion and Action," the incontinent Mr. Burke
presents himself in the guise of a valetudinarian friend with a
weak bladder who is especially interested "in the thinking of the
body as it affects the imagery of poetry" and who acts on the
assumption that "*all* bodily processes must have their effect upon
human imagery if men are to avoid the charge of 'angelism,' that
is, the claim to think, like angels, in ways purely intellectualistic,
without the intervention of bodily imagination."[3] As might be
predicted, Burke eventually considers the disquisition of the
drunken Porter in *Macbeth* on the effects of alcohol on the
human body. It provokes "nose-painting, sleep, and urine. Lech-
ery, sir, it provokes, and unprovokes; it provokes the desire, but it
takes away the performance." For the rest, literary criticism has
not had much to say about the relationship between body imagery
and poetic imagery unless it has been informed by psychoanalysis—as Burke's is.[4]

3. Kenneth Burke, *Language as Symbolic Action* (Berkeley: University of
California Press, 1968), p. 345.

4. In this connection I might mention that Stanley Burnshaw's *The Seamless
Web* (New York: George Braziller, 1970) opens by saying, "Poetry begins with
the body and ends with the body" (p. 1). See also the compendious footnote (no. 70)
on body imagery in poetry in Angus Fletcher, *Allegory* (Ithaca: Cornell University
Press, 1964), p. 114. Since writing the original draft of this chapter I have en-
countered an excellent book paralleling and complementing what I say in this chapter in a variety of ways: Cary Nelson, *The Incarnate Word: Literature as Verbal
Space* (Urbana: University of Illinois Press, 1973). Nelson's exploration of the
nature of verbal space claims that "to read is to fold the world into the body's
house" (p. 6).

Scarcely literary criticism, but more relevant at this point than any other work for appreciating the overwhelming importance of the human body in human arts and institutions, is the cosmology that is *Love's Body*. At times Norman O. Brown's treatment of body imagery can be exasperating: "All metaphors are sexual; a penis in every convex object and a vagina in every concave one," he says. Even a confirmed Freudian might want to argue with Brown's global generalization by asking the shape of the images in T. S. Eliot's

> let their liquid siftings fall
> To stain the stiff dishonored shroud.

But the joke is on us if we fall into the trap of reading *Love's Body* in a literal way. As Brown says, everything is symbolic—including the activities of people who write about convex and concave metaphors. "Literalism makes the world of abstract materialism; of dead matter, of the human body as dead matter. Literalism kills everything, including the human body" (p. 223). Whatever its limitations, a major accomplishment of Brown's revolutionary book is to flesh out the flesh-garment of language. "The word is made flesh. To recover the world of silence, of symbolism, is to recover the human body" (p. 265). Then Brown quotes Ella Freeman Sharpe once again: "A subterranean passage between mind and body underlies all analogy." He adds, "The true meanings of words are bodily meanings, carnal knowledge; and the bodily meanings are the unspoken meanings. What is always speaking silently is the body."

As the incantatory, mesmeric prose of the King James Bible intones, "In the beginning was the Word, and the Word was with God, and the Word was God" (John 1:1). And in time, "The Word was made flesh, and dwelt among us (and we beheld his glory, the glory as the only begotten of the Father) full of grace and truth" (John 1:14). Thus the essential and abstract and uncorporeal God became flesh, became concrete and alive in the hearts and minds of men. The word is made flesh by the poet who makes the reader believe by making the words come alive. Yet at the same time the word is made flesh, the flesh is made into words. The words of the poet are flesh-made. They grow out of his body, the needs of his body, and their vitality for the reader

lies in the needs of *his* body. Poet and reader experience their
bodily needs in words. If words and their meanings do not spring
from the loins, the words of poetry cannot be made flesh. They
will be quarried from dictionaries, and stone dead.

The mind confuses tenor and vehicle. In speaking of the word
made flesh I speak figuratively, yet the word is made flesh—or at
least this process is facilitated—by the poet's reference to actual
parts of the body. One thing leads to another. When Juliet says
"palm to palm is holy palmer's kiss," a romance has been
launched in the mind of the reader. As for Juliet's metaphor, she
only turns things around. Palm trees take their name from the
leaves fanning out like the palm of a human hand (from the
Latin, *palma*). Juliet makes several transfers. One is from the
palm fronds of the pilgrim to the palm of a hand. Another is
palm to palm as a metaphor for kissing. Still another is from a
touching that is a kissing to a kissing that leads to and symbolizes
another way of joining bodies—for Romeo and Juliet have more
than holding hands in mind. And finally, Juliet rarifies a bodily
metaphor into a spiritual one, ritualizing and sanctifying the
various forms of connection. The needs of the body speak through
the body of language which is the language of the body to the
extent that it is informed by or infused with its own subject: the
needs of the body. We cannot even utter the word "language"
without using and referring to the human body.

Every image has at least a trace of sensuousness in it, according to C. Day Lewis, "even the most purely emotional or intellectual one," and later he notes that there must be some relationship
between the evocative power of images and their sensuous elements.[5] Almost every cluster of metaphors examined thus far has
been rooted in the element of sensuousness, from Keats's ripe
plum, fingering its misty bloom, to the finger of St. Joseph in
Yeats's "A Stick of Incense." The presence of clusters of body
imagery tends to cue the reader in such a way as to mobilize his
primary-process activity. That activity then becomes part of the
developing modal ambiguity that provides the dynamics for deep,
complex responses to poetry's full range of meaning, as I have
tried to show earlier.

5. C. Day Lewis, *The Poetic Image,* pp. 19 and 41.

By way of emphasizing the dynamic function of sensuous elements in poetry in their role of promoting deeper, fuller, more erotic responses to language, I will quote—in order of increasing psychological complexity—some familiar poetry which happens to be redolent with body imagery. A classic example of exquisite appeal to the senses can be found in this stanza of Ben Jonson from "The Triumph of Charis":

> Have you seen but a bright lily grow
>   Before rude hands have touched it?
> Ha' you marked but the fall o' the snow
>   Before the soil hath smutched it?
> Ha' you felt the wool of beaver
>   Or swan's down ever?
> Or have smelt o' the bud o' the brier?
>   Or the nard in the fire?
> Or have tasted the bag of the bee?
> O so white, O so soft, O so sweet is she!

Perfect in terms of what it tries to accomplish, such imagery epitomizes the sensuous particularity most of us tend to think of as an essential feature of poetic discourse.

Quite as charming in its sensuous appeal but illustrating a fuller range of sensibility is the passage from "Sleep and Poetry" where Keats envisions the first stage in his career as a poet of the highest aspiration:

>   First the realm I'll pass
> Of Flora and old Pan: sleep in the grass,
> Feed upon apples red, and strawberries,
> And choose each pleasure that my fancy sees;
> Catch the white-handed nymphs in shady places,
> Too woo sweet kisses from averted faces,—
> Play with their fingers, touch their shoulders white
> Into a pretty shrinking with a bite
> As hard as lips can make it: till agreed,
> A lovely tale of human life we'll read.

Here we have the interchangeability of the word made flesh and the flesh made word. Keats writes about writing poetry. As an "objective correlative" for expressing what he will write and how he will write it he may be said to use his subject as object and his object as subject, infusing his fantasy about writing poetry with the very fantasy material that will suffuse the poetry. Similar in

their perfection of ornamental detail are these rich lines from
"Epithalamion," by the poet Keats began by imitating—Edmund
Spenser. They describe his bride as

> Adorned with beautyes grace and vertues store,
> Her goodly eyes lyke Saphyres shining bright,
> Her forehead yvory white,
> Her cheekes lyke apples which the sun hath rudded,
> Her lips lyke cherryes charming men to byte,
> Her brest like to a bowle of creame uncrudded,
> Her paps lyke lyllies budded,
> Her snowie necke lyke to a marble towre,
> And all her body like a pallace fayre,
> Ascending uppe with many a stately stayre,
> To honors seat and chastities sweet bowre.

A poet of strength as well as delicacy, Spenser lets go with bolder
lines from time to time to further enliven his nuptial song, as
when he counsels abandonment of restraint at the feast with
these words:

> Poure out the wine without restraint or stay,
> Poure not by cups, but by the belly full,
> Poure out to all that wull,
> And sprinkle all the postes and wals with wine,
> That they may sweat, and drunken be withall.

I know my own experience of these lines would be inferior had
Spenser said something like "Poure not by cups, but by the barrel
full" instead of "by the belly full."

At roughly this point in the poem, though there can be no
sharp dividing line, the language of Spenser moves beyond a
simple sensuous (and sensual) appeal and begins to operate more
fully in the service of imagination. Though without the loveliness
of images like "forehead yvory white" and "cheekes lyke apples"
and "brest like to a bowle of creame uncrudded," the lines about
the walls drunk with sweat in sympathy for the proceedings are
less literal. They have more reach, more tension, more of what
Hopkins would call "instress." Nor is it just a question of employing the pathetic fallacy, either, though it may be that now we can
better understand the strange force this rhetorical device can
have in the hands of a substantial poet. Wil we, nil we, lines like
"sprinkle all the postes and wals with wine,/That they may

sweat, and drunken be withall" make us *feel* the joy and release, the spirit of revelry. There's something more primitive, almost glandular about our response to the words.

Shakespeare's mature period gives us this picture of a beautiful young maiden blushing, when Florizel whispers to Perdita:

> He tells her something
> That makes her blood look out. Good sooth, she is
> The queen of curds and cream.

The corporeality of these lines is such that one part of the body metaphors another part: Perdita's blood looks out. John Donne creates a vignette of a blushing maiden almost as impressive in "The Second Anniversary":

> Wee understood
> Her by her sight; her pure, and eloquent blood
> Spoke in her cheekes, and so distinctly wrought,
> That one might almost say, her body thought.

The body does think, as Burke will have it in the title of his paper on catharsis imagery, and Donne himself speaks, in "The Blossome," of his "naked thinking heart." There has been much to-do of late in popular psychology about "body language" and the revelations we make through posture and carriage. Half the job of an actor is to learn how to make such revelations. And in ballet this kind of ripeness is all.

Because of what Ella Freeman Sharpe calls the subterranean passage between mind and body underlying all analogy, there may be no single source of poetic imagery with as much potential for disturbing the reader as the human body. When Marina wishes to vent the fullness of her disgust to Boult, she says, "Thy food is such / As hath been belched on by infected lungs" (*Pericles* 4.6.179). In a lighter vein, William Blake voices political anger after he has the King of France declare how loath he is to execute his subjects:

> Then old Nobodaddy aloft
> Farted & belch'd & cough'd,
> And said, "I love hanging & drawing & quartering
> Every bit as well as war & slaughtering."

In one of the great short poems of the language, "Infant Sorrow," Blake expresses an absolutely primal kind of bodily awareness:

> My mother groan'd! my father wept.
> Into the dangerous world I leapt:
> Helpless, naked, piping loud:
> Like a fiend hid in a cloud.
>
> Struggling in my father's hands,
> Striving against my swadling bands.
> Bound and weary I thought best
> To sulk upon my mother's breast.

The metaphors that matter here are what I call "naive": the mother's groans, the father's tears, and the rest. They do not look like metaphors at all in their deceptive simplicity. And it is part of the deceptiveness of the simplicity of Blake's language here that he so effortlessly conjures up for us the sense of what it feels like to be born—and into such a world. One reason why Blake can wring so much feeling from seemingly flat images is that he knows that "Energy is the only life, and is from the Body" ("The Marriage of Heaven and Hell"). This kind of energy bursts at the seams of "The Tyger," as in these lines:

> And what the shoulder, & what art,
> Could twist the sinews of thy heart?
> And when thy heart began to beat,
> What dread hand? & what dread feet?

I can recall how odd this poem used to seem to me, even after many readings, but now I know the kernel of rightness and familiarity within the husk of its strangeness lies in the corporeality of the imagery.

We are told by St. Gregory the Great why the diction of the "Song of Songs" is carnal language. "In this book love is expressed as if in carnal language so that the mind, stimulated by words it is accustomed to . . . may be aroused from its torpor, and through words concerned with a love that is below, may be excited to a love which is above."[6] Whatever one may say about St. Gregory's hermeneutics, his psychology is sound. Sound, too, is the instinct of faith expressing itself through the familiar language of the body so often exhibited elsewhere in the scriptures, as in the Book of Job: "Naked came I out of my mother's womb, and naked shall I return thither" (1:21), and "Why died I

6. Quoted in D. W. Robertson, *A Preface to Chaucer* (Princeton: Princeton University Press, 1962), p. 28.

not from the womb? why did I not give up the ghost when I came out of the belly?" (3:11). What I remember most vividly among Job's many afflictions are the boils. "My flesh is clothed with worms and clods of dust; my skin is broken, and become loathsome." Job, sitting in the ashes, scraping his skin with a potsherd —in such details as these lies the poetry of his abject condition. Consider in the same vein the spirituality in the physiology of Psalm 22:

> My God, my God, why hast thou forsaken me? why art thou so far from helping me, and from the words of my roaring? O my God, I cry in the daytime, but thou hearest not; and in the night season, and am not silent. But thou art holy O thou that inhabitest the praises of Israel. Our fathers trusted in thee: they trusted, and thou didst deliver them. They cried unto thee, and were delivered: they trusted in thee, and were not confounded. But I am a worm, and no man; a reproach of men, and despised of the people. All they that see me laugh me to scorn: they shoot out the lip, they shake the head, saying, He trusted on the LORD that he would deliver him: let him deliver him, seeing he delighted in him. But thou art he that took me out of the womb: thou art my God from my mother's belly. Be not far from me; for trouble is near; for there is none to help. Many bulls have encompassed me; strong bulls of Bashan have beset me round. They gaped upon me with their mouths, as a ravening and roaring lion. I am poured out like water, and all my bones are out of joint: my heart is like wax; it is melted in the midst of my bowels. My strength is dried up like a potsherd; and my tongue cleaveth to my jaws; and thou hast brought me into the dust of death. For dogs have compassed me: the assembly of the wicked have inclosed me: they pierced my hands and feet.

The last image of these humble and familiar words remind us of the most influential of all body metaphors: the crucifixion.

Poets instinctively turn to images of the body when they mean to disturb the reader most. Whether T. S. Eliot means to shock his readers into an attitude of spiritual awareness or merely retches up some of his own emotional vomitus, he contrives in "Sweeney Erect" to parody the contortions of sexual ecstasy through the convulsions of epilepsy, the curse of one of Mrs. Turner's girls in the whorehouse:

> This withered root of knots of hair
>   Slitted below and gashed with eyes,
> This oval O cropped out with teeth:
>   The sickle motion from the thighs
>
> Jackknifes upward at the knees
>   Then straightens out from heel to hip
> Pushing the framework of the bed
>   And clawing at the pillow slip.

But it is not from Sweeney's point of view that the girl's shrieking mouth becomes a vagina dentata. As he develops a parallel of spiritual numbness, Eliot creates a perfect contrast here between the bestial agony of the prostitute and the bestial equanimity of Sweeney by relying heavily on physiology in both cases. Sweeney erect remains untroubled by such visions, immune to agony:

> Sweeney addressed full length to shave
>   Broadbottomed, pink from nape to base,
> Knows the female temperament
>   And wipes the suds around his face.
>
> (The lengthened shadow of a man
>   Is history, said Emerson
> Who had not seen the silhouette
>   Of Sweeney straddled in the sun.)

Eliot has a genius rivalling that of Hieronymus Bosch for dwelling on the more leperous possibilities of the human anatomy, as these stanzas from "Whispers of Immortality" reveal:

> Webster was much possessed by death
> And saw the skull beneath the skin;
> And breastless creatures under ground
> Leaned backward with a lipless grin.
>
>   Daffodil bulbs instead of balls
> Stared from the sockets of the eyes!
> He knew that thought clings round dead limbs
> Tightening its lusts and luxuries.

If more poets were doctors, like William Carlos Williams, it would surprise no one to find bards dissecting bodies in search of fresh metaphors. One might even expect to find an astonishing number of body tropes in view of the intricacy of human anatomy. The wonder is that so few parts can be made to do so much service. Poets are not technicians. They have no care for capillaries. There are only a few bones, a dozen organs, a hank of hair here and a patch of skin there, that they pay much attention to. But all poets worthy of the name do pay attention to the body in one way or another, one part or another.

Why? The question is rhetorical. Psychoanalysis has always insisted on the primacy of the body in developmental matters. There is no question genetically, of which came first, body or mind. We have bodies first, minds afterwards. We are made by bodies, born out of bodies, born with bodies, and we bear these bodies with us to the grave. The body is basic. It is not all there is to life, but it is where it all begins. And where it all ends: sans teeth, sans eyes, sans taste, sans everything.

Our very sense of selfhood begins with the drawing of boundaries between our "body ego" and the rest of the world, especially between Self and Other (self-object differentiation), the process Margaret Mahler calls "individuation."[7] Because of the vastness of the psychoanalytic literature bearing in one way or another on the relationship of mind and body, my references to such work must be highly selective.[8] I would therefore like to return, first of all, to that most willing breast of essays on metaphor and psychology, Ella Freeman Sharpe's "An Examination of Metaphor." After speaking of the subterranean passage between mind and body underlying all analogy, Sharpe offers the example of a husband coaching his wife about trouble caused by the incontinence of their son's bowels. "Of course you feel angry, that's natural, but don't let John see your anger," he says. "Think to yourself you must keep your anger in and hold it in till you get to another room and then you can let it out." The son will have to learn similar control over urine and feces, says Sharpe; he will have to learn to hold things in until he gets to another room. When control over bodily apertures becomes stabilized, bodily discharges can take other forms.

7. Margaret Mahler, *On Human Symbiosis and the Vicissitudes of Individuation* (New York: International Universities Press, 1968), vol. I.

8. See Paul Schilder, *The Image and Appearance of the Human Body* (New York: International Universities Press, 1960); Seymour Fisher and Sidney E. Cleveland, *Body Image and Personality* (Princeton: Van Nostrand, 1958); and Felix Deutsch, *Body, Mind, and the Sensory Gateways* (New York: Basic Books, 1962).

At the same time as sphincter control over anus and urethra is being established, the child is acquiring the power of speech, and an avenue of "outer-ance" present from birth becomes of immense importance. First of all the discharge of feeling tension, when this is no longer relieved by physical discharge, can take place through speech. The activity of speaking is substituted for the physical activity now restricted at other openings of the body, while words themselves become the very substitutes for the bodily substances. Speech secondly becomes a way of expressing, discharging ideas. So that we may say speech in itself is a metaphor. [p. 157]

To say that speech can be a symbolic substitute for other forms of bodily discharge, often in an almost one-to-one fashion, does not of course mean that all language is a veiled form of micturation or defecation. It will not do to divide all such language phenomena into morbid and nonmorbid, as Robert Fliess does in his discussion of erogenic language.[9] The division by Fliess of all utterance into "speech" (ideational) and "language" (affective) leads him to make too many gross equivalencies, like "silence must be considered as the equivalent of sphincter closure." As any good clinician knows, silences in therapy may have many kinds of meaning. They can even signify the emergence of a warm, loving, symbiotic phase of the interaction. What we have in the overdetermined language of poetry is not some uneasy mixture of morbid and nonmorbid material but rather a fusion of regressive material with highly developed ideas, values, and so on—that is, language geared to the full mentational spectrum.

Sharpe explains metaphor in terms of function as well as genesis. The main function of libidinalized speech is discharge, getting outside what is bottled up inside. Some common nonverbal modes of bodily discharge include laughing, sighing, and crying. Spitting can be a spontaneous symbol of disgust. Vomiting can be hysterical. Sweating, while normally just part of the body's cooling system, can be a sign of nervousness, as can other excretory processes. Respiratory functions and malfunctions, like asthma, can have an expressive dimension. There are all kinds of psychogenic tics and twitches. Even coughing can fall into this category. Psychosomatic symptoms such as eczema are legion.

9. Robert Fliess, *Erotgeneity and Libido* (New York: International Universities Press, 1956), chapter 7.

Epileptic seizures, if Freud is right, can articulate that complex of thought and feeling called a death-wish.[10] And perhaps the most obviously psychosomatic of all modes of discharge is orgasm. What all of these somatic "expressions," or body metaphors, have in common with the primary process is that they are, or may be, modes of discharging psychic energy. The communicational primitiveness of these coordinate expressions of psyche and soma hark back to an early, generalized, diffuse or undifferentiated modality of perception (and expression) René Spitz labels *coenesthetic reception,* in which the infant responds with great sensitivity to such cues from the sensorium as equilibrium, temperature, skin contact, rhythm, voice timbre, and the like.[11]

Freud mentions that hysterical patients suffer from reminiscences. He compares their conversion symptoms with "mnemic symbols" of traumatic historical events, like the monument at Charing Cross.[12] The symptom "memorializes" a painful event. Freud also speaks about how highly charged with emotion the physical symptom can be. In this respect, hysterical symptoms are physiological metaphors—highly condensed "statements" of the body's pains and desires. In poetry, emotion gets in*corp*orated in language, especially in body imagery. A curious little prose poem entitled "Hysteria" portrays a nameless woman overwhelmed by laughter. It begins,

> As she laughed I was aware of becoming involved in her laughter and being part of it, until her teeth were only accidental stars with a talent for squaddrill. I was drawn in by short gasps, inhaled at each momentary recovery, lost finally in the dark caverns of her throat, bruised by the ripple of unseen muscles.

These lines by T. S. Eliot illustrate how strong emotions can momentarily usurp control of the musculature. They reveal more than that. The irony of Eliot's hyperbole does not succeed in damping the anxiety resulting from the speaker's sense of being engulfed in the woman's oral cavity, a perilous engulfment depicted as parturition in reverse.

10. "Dostoevsky and Parricide," *Std. Ed.,* XXI, pp. 173-96.
11. René Spitz, *The First Year of Life* (New York: International Universities Press, 1965), p. 134. Spitz remarks that "the relation between the coenesthetic and diacritic organizations is reminiscent of that between primary and secondary process."
12. "Five Lectures on Psycho-Analysis," *Std. Ed.,* XI, pp. 16-18.

Mental trips into body functions of similar profundity are sometimes made when imagination receives chemical assistance. A subject under LSD reports a "powerful sense of the whole evolutionary process. This process is symbolized by an incredibly long snake that extends back through time from the present to the beginnings of all life. The snake is seen as an image but S also *feels* himself, his body, to *be* what he is imagining."[13] This report might be re-interpreted as involving ontogenesis in the guise of phylogenesis. If the snake is fecal, or umbilical, the report expresses a psychophysiological fantasy of the subject's own birth, or rebirth, during the state of deep regression promoted by the ingestion of LSD. The authors of the book containing this report inform us in a chapter entitled "Experiencing the Body and the Body Image" that the subject of psychedelic phenomena may "experience slight or drastic changes in the size, configuration, substance, weight and other attributes contributing to definition of the body. He may seem to himself to assume the form of some animal or even some inanimate object; and he may be reduced to a subatomic particle or expanded to the proportions of a galaxy. He may experience his body's dissolution and the sense of having no body at all—the so-called somatopsychic depersonalization" (p. 68). The "connection" to be made in this context lies in the significance the experiences of poetry and drugs have in common. Each kind of experience must be essentially psychological and at least partially regressive. While response to certain drugs may have more pronounced physiological concomitants, as might be expected, the experience of poetry can no more be divorced from the deeper heritage of the body than taking hallucinogens can be divorced from the participation of the central nervous system.

Another basis for arguing the vital role body imagery has in mobilizing primary-process mentation can be found in the recent work of John Bowlby.[14] Beginning as a student of separation anxiety, Bowlby has now become the chief exponent in psychoanalytic circles of the view that early ties are characterized not so much by their nurturant aspect, which may be called the Cookie

13. R. E. L. Masters and Jean Houston, *The Varieties of Psychedelic Experience* (New York: Dell, 1966), p. 30.
14. John Bowlby, *Attachment* (New York: Basic Books, 1969) and *Separation* (New York: Basic Books, 1973).

Jar Theory of Dependency, as by sheer attachment, attachment behavior that seems to be instinctive in nature and largely independent of nurturance, or what is usually called orality. Drawing on ethological studies as well as the observation of human infants, Bowlby stresses the fundamental importance of a young monkey's impulse to cling tightly to his mother's body in any fear-provoking situation. He also points to the well-known experiments H. F. Harlow has done in showing how monkeys deprived of real mothers will cling to cloth surrogates—and even to surrogates made of wire in the absence of anything more comforting. If imprinting takes place during the optimal period, attachments to mothering figures can be so profound as to cross the barrier of species, as in the remarkable instance in which Konrad Lorenz beguiled newly hatched mallard ducklings into following him around as though he were their natural mother. The point to be registered is that attachment does not occur in a corporal vacuum. People spend most of their lives clinging to one another, in one way or another—and of course sometimes at several removes, where the attachment is to pets, money, material goods, or rituals. Whatever forms they take, from an hierarchical point of view these attachments must necessarily hark back to an original clinging of one body to another.

Perhaps the clearest way of all to emphasize the profound relationship between the primary process and corporality is to look at psychosis as a meeting place of mind and body. The presence of primary-process mentation does not by itself define psychosis, nor is there anything necessarily psychotic inherent in the operations of the primary process. What the two have so much in common is a preoccupation with bodily concerns. Consider, for instance, the unlabelled metaphor of Leon, a paranoid schizophrenic who believes himself to be Christ incarnate. He says, "If I hate another person, I rip myself part." Leon means this statement literally. When he utters his hatred of his mother, only a splintered portion of his whole self may be said to speak:

> She's not my mother. I sincerely know from experience that she's an old witch, a devil, a duper. She is in with the arsenic and old lace gang. . . . A woman bore me; she consented to having me killed electronically while she was bearing me, which is in itself a disowning of a child. And I disowned her after I put the picture together. . . . It's true what people say about her, when I was

growing up, that she was a first-class fornicator, that she's no good, that she's worse than trash. That particular woman, I call her the Old Witch, because only an old witch would consent to doing a thing she has done. She's a disfigured midget. . . . She's a murderer. I had the occasion of almost being killed by her through arsenic that she put in the food and drink. . . . Can such a thing really happen? It did happen, sir, and many other things such as sucking and blowing me off after putting knockout drops in my food. And when she does such things, as far as I'm concerned she's an old witch; she's not my mother.[15]

Much like Dr. Schreber's experience of his punitive father, Leon may be said to have experienced his mother's ministrations (or lack of them) in the form of paranoid delusions of attacks upon his body.

Conversely, the mending of such grave fissures of the mind and spirit will necessarily involve repair of the body ego. In the remarkable case of Renee, discussed by Marguerite Sechehaye in *Symbolic Realization* and by the patient herself in *Autobiography of a Schizophrenic Girl,* Renee attempts, in her delusional states, to carry out the punitive orders of "The System" by starving herself. When the therapy finally begins to be effective, one facet of treatment is for Renee to explore and learn to love her own body by taking warm baths. Another is to have the experience of good mothering in symbolic form, such as by eating apples representing her analyst's breasts. "Though Renee was developing in autonomous ego on the oral level, she was still not clearly cognizant of having a body, of being a body," Sechehaye says of one stage of the recovery. "For the ego is equally a body ego. . . . Like a small child, Renee did not imagine herself one with her own body, as proof of which she referred to her body as to an object independent of, though linked to, her; and when any part ailed, she at once objectified it, isolating it from the rest. As a result she did not say, 'My arm hurts,' but 'the arm is sick,' quite as though it were an independent thing, thereby removing the arm as far from her body as possible."[16]

15. Milton Rokeach, *The Three Christs of Ypsilanti* (New York: Vintage, 1964), pp. 75, 78-79.

16. M. A. Sechehaye, *Symbolic Realization* (New York: International Universities Press, 1951); *Autobiography of a Schizophrenic Girl,* Grace Rubin-Rabson, trans., with analytic interpretation by Marguerite Sechehaye (New York: Signet, 1970), pp. 112-13.

No clinical material I know of better illustrates the extent to which integrity of the body self underlies the integrity of the behavioral self than the extraordinary case of Susan, the schizophrenic young woman described by Marion Milner in *The Hands of the Living God*.[17] Susan begins one session by telling a dream she feels must mean she will never get well: "She saw a figure with arms and legs all over the place, kind of floating, and a breast somewhere." This disjointedness of her body image appears in hundreds of the drawings Susan produces during the course of therapy. One is of a face that looks like a rectum. The next drawing Milner discusses appears to her as a picture of a cavity, "not of a face, but a cavity which has some kind of sentience, since it has the basic features of a profile face on its inner boundary—but it also has teeth-like forms all round it. In fact, could it not be an attempt to depict the idea of an anus-vagina as a biting-off organ; or, to put it in another way, is there not here a primitive conception in which mouth, vagina, and anus are all undifferentiated?" One day Susan brings one of the many alternating-profile pictures she draws that collapse both frontal and profile views: "Here there are either two oval faces in profile with their noses pressed close together, or a whole full face with a mouth and drops of saliva, although it can also be read as buttocks emitting faeces. Alternatively, the eyes in the middle of the two ovals can be seen as the nipples of two breasts." Milner interprets this drawing as including "not only the identification of mouth and anus, breasts and buttocks, but also, because of the loving way in which the two profiles meet, the idea that she can give back to me, with her faeces, in return for what she gets from my 'breasts,' and therefore perhaps feel it is safe to feel her mouth watering excitedly for 'food' because she does have something to give back."

The intimate relationship of soma to psyche appears in its most dramatic manifestations through the distorting mirror of psychotic thought processes. This relationship can be seen almost at a glance in pictorial form in the pages of books on psychotic art, where virtually every painting, drawing, and sculpture reflects

17. Marion Milner, *The Hands of the Living God* (New York: International Universities Press, 1969), pp. 109, 127, 200.

serious impairment of the body ego, representations which ought
not to be confused with deliberate, playful variations on the
subject of somatic form and space such as one encounters in the
statues of Henry Moore, or the comic drawings of Daumier, or
the savage satire of Goya's *Capriccios.* As for the essentially
nonvisual medium of poetry, I can think of no one whose writing
better serves to illustrate the connectedness of soma and psyche
than Sylvia Plath.

In the schizoid entanglements of her work the emotions of
love and hate are so entwined that only her final, fatal, savage
attack on her own body could resolve the dispute.[18] What most of
all serves to involve her readers in her agony is the extent to
which they can share bodies with her in imagination because of the
way her imagery promotes the primary process. Any reader,
regardless of gender and sexual identity, can empathize with the
opening lines of a poem like "Cut":

> What a thrill—
> My thumb instead of an onion.
> The top quite gone
> Except for a sort of a hinge
>
> Of skin,
> A flap like a hat,
> Dead white.

As in many of her poems, the theme here has to do with the
vulnerability of the body and its boundaries to damage.

While nothing that could be labelled distortion of the body
image appears in this poem, hints of the beginning of Sylvia
Plath's grotesque variations on her own sense of body space seem
to be foreshadowed in her representations of her parents' bodies.
Her attitudes toward the bodies of the two most important
people in the world can be found in "Sow" and "The Colossus,"
the latter serving as the title of her first volume of poems.
Mingled awe and hatred of the Primal Mother lurks behind the
comic tone of "Sow":

18. My speculations about Plath's mind and language have in part been
stimulated and guided by an article entitled "The Absence at the Center: Sylvia
Plath and Suicide" by my colleagues, Christopher Bollas and Murray Schwartz,
published in *Criticism* XVIII (Spring, 1976): 147-72.

> God knows how our neighbor managed to breed
> His great sow:
> Whatever his shrewd secret, he kept it hid
>
> In the same way
> He kept the sow—impounded from public stare,
> Prize ribbon and pig show.

One night the children are allowed to gape at what threatens to become a primal scene:

> This was no rose-and-larkspurred china suckling
> With a penny slot
>
> For thrifty children, nor dolt pig ripe for heckling
> About to be
> Glorified for prime flesh and golden crackling
>
> In a parsley halo;
> Nor even one of the common barnyard sows,
> Mire-smirched, blowzy,
>
> Maunching thistle and knotweed on her snout-cruise—
> Bloat tun of milk
> On the move, hedged by a litter of feat-foot ninnies
>
> Shrilling her hulk
> To halt for a swing at the pink teats. No. This vast
> Brobdingnag bulk
>
> Of a sow lounged belly-bedded on that black compost,
> Fat-rutted eyes
> Dream-filmed. What a vision of ancient hoghood must
>
> Thus wholly engross
> The great grandam!—our marvel blazoned a knight,
> Helmed, in cuirass,
>
> Unhorsed and shredded in the grove of combat
> By a grisly-bristled
> Boar, fabulous enough to straddle that sow's heat.

It would take a colossus of a boar to do that, and that colossal daddy, particularly the daughter's infantile feelings about his body, get described in "The Colossus." It begins:

> I shall never get you put together entirely,
> Pieced, glued, and properly jointed,
> Mule-bray, pig-grunt and bawdy cackles
> Proceed from your great lips.
> It's worse than a barnyard.

Perhaps, she thinks, he is some god or other, some mouthpiece of
the dead, but gets no answer.

> Thirty years now I have labored
> To dredge the silt from your throat.
> I am none the wiser.
>
> Scaling little ladders with gluepots and pails of lysol
> I crawl like an ant in mourning
> Over the weedy acres of your brow
> To mend the immense skull plates and clear
> The bald, white tumuli of your eyes.

Throughout the poem Plath's time-capsuled impressions of her
father's hulking proportions—as seen from her eyes as a little
girl—get translated into body metaphors that express his emotional importance for her. Toward the end of the poem she says,

> Nights, I squat in the cornucopia
> Of your left ear, out of the wind.
>
> Counting the red stars and those of plum-color.
> The sun rises under the pillar of your tongue.

Sylvia Plath repeatedly creates analogues of the psychological
stature of her father in the form of make-believe representations
of the physiological gigantesque, so that it is not surprising to
find "Daddy" opening with these body images:

> You do not do, you do not do
> Any more, black shoe
> In which I have lived like a foot
> For thirty years, poor and white,
> Barely daring to breathe or Achoo.
>
> Daddy, I have had to kill you.
> You died before I had time—
> Marble-heavy, a bag full of God,
> Ghastly statue with one grey toe
> Big as a Frisco seal

Among the most poignant of her poems are those reflecting
her own body ego, especially those in which her feelings do not
add up to anything like basic trust in the availability of her body
as a vital, integral, meaningful, pleasure-possible gestalt. One of
these poems is "The Stones," set in a hospital "city" and descriptive of the condensed feelings of a body exposed to the traumata

of chronic sinusitis, apendectomy, childbirth, miscarriage, and the sense of physical dissolution resulting from her attempted suicide. In the poem she feels like a stone. She describes the ministrations of the hospital personnel:

> The food tubes embrace me. Sponges kiss my lichens away.
> The jewelmaster drives his chisel to pry
> Open one stone eye.
>
> This is the after-hell: I see the light.
> A wind unstoppers the chamber
> Of the ear, old worrier.
>
> Water mollifies the flint lip,
> And daylight lays its sameness on the wall.
> The grafters are cheerful,
>
> Heating the pincers, hoisting the delicate hammers,
> A current agitates the wires
> Volt upon volt. Catgut stitches my fissures.
>
> A workman walks by carrying a pink torso.
> The storerooms are full of hearts.
> This is the city of spare parts.

In another hospital poem, "Tulips," we are told that "The tulips are too red in the first place, they hurt me." She hears them breathe and feels they "eat my oxygen." The tulips have eyes, tongues, faces

> And I have no face, I have wanted to efface myself.

She has the schizoid thin, papery feeling.

Usually it is possible to distinguish between neurotic and psychotic art. As Ernst Kris suggests, in the former case the primary process operates in the service of the ego whereas in psychotic art the primary process overwhelms the ego. In Sylvia Plath's poetry it is sometimes difficult to decide where the boundaries are. In "Tulips," for example, the title of the poem reflects Plath's obsession with the theme of devouring mouths by utilizing what can only be called a clang association: two-lips. Unlike an ordinary pun, this play on the identical sounds of the two images functions so as to confuse rather than compare. As distinct from an Aristotelean "transfer," the lipped mouths of the tulips present the reader with a piece of aural boundarylessness in the undifferentiated flux of primary-process mentation. In "Tulips" there can also be found a schizoid reversal of the animate and inanimate, a shift reminiscent of Sechehaye's patient's experience of the inanimate world, like the wind, as literally alive while her sense of real people was that they had become robots. "Tulips" represents a severe emotional depletion of the speaker's family relationships by depicting their attachment to her as involving smiles that are depersonalized and thing-like:

> My husband and child smiling out of the family photo;
> Their smiles catch onto my skin, little smiling hooks.

Emotion and ideation become completely somatized at times in schizophrenia. Harold Searles writes of a patient who spoke of what seemed to her some hurtful words from her doctor as being like a bullet through her heart, and he explains that such statements are not mere metaphors but somatic equivalents for the patient's emotion.[19] In a comparable instance a patient of Searles interprets his disjointed posture as body language signifying his intent to dismember her! Smiles as skin-catching hooks, and oxygen-stealing tulips seem to me to illustrate this kind of somatization of emotion.

The poem called "Lady Lazarus" voices the pathos, the agony, and the destructive fury of Sylvia Plath's suicide attempt through a series of images of her body, the only adequate "vehicle" for the expression of such horrifying emotions. It begins,

> I have done it again.
> One year in every ten
> I manage it—
>
> A sort of walking miracle, my skin
> Bright as a Nazi lampshade,
> My right foot
>
> A paperweight,
> My face a featureless, fine
> Jew linen.

After these images attacking her father for his Nazi leanings, she speaks of the flesh the "grave cave ate" and then of "the big strip tease" before a peanut-munching crowd when her rescuers pull

19. Harold F. Searles, *Collected Papers on Schizophrenia*, p. 582.

her out from under the house three days after she swallows fifty
sleeping pills:

> Gentleman, ladies,
>
> These are my hands,
> My knees.
> I may be skin and bone,
>
> Nevertheless, I am the same, identical woman.
> The first time it happened I was ten.
> It was an accident.
>
> The second time I meant
> To last it out and not come back at all.
> I rocked shut
>
> As a seashell.
> They had to call and call
> And pick the worms off me like sticky pearls.

According to Bollas and Schwartz her suicide means, among
other things, a turning-against-the-self of homicidal anger toward her father.[20] An intimation of this equivalence appears at
the end of "Lady Lazarus" when, once again identifying with
Ariel, she threatens the enemy Father:

> Herr God, Herr Lucifer,
> Beware
> Beware.
>
> Out of the ash
> I rise with my red hair
> And I eat men like air.

She eats gas in the end, gas from her own oven. Shortly before
that event, when all her fantasies press in the direction of self-
destruction, she articulates her deepest longing in "Poppies in
July," a poem filled with images of masochistic yearning for
liberation by death.

> Little poppies, little hell flames,
> Do you do no harm?
>
> You flicker. I cannot touch you.
> I put my hands among the flames. Nothing burns.

20. "Absence at the Center," p. 155.

This denial immediately gives way to an expression of utter
emotional depletion:

And it exhausts me to watch you
Flickering like that, wrinkly and clear red, like the skin of a mouth.

In a flash this thought opens up a Pandora's box of obsessive
thoughts condensed into a few words:

> A mouth just bloodied.
> Little bloody skirts!
>
> There are fumes that I cannot touch.
> Where are your opiates, your nauseous capsules?
>
> If I could bleed, or sleep!—
> If my mouth could marry a hurt like that!
>
> Or your liquors seep to me, in this glass capsule,
> Dulling and stilling.

The poem culminates in this image for Nirvana:

> But colourless. Colourless.

It cannot be accidental that the poem takes the form of an
apostrophe. Sylvia Plath addresses the poppies. In actuality she
directs her words of pain to her mother (not to her "real" mother
but to that imagined psychological good mother for whom she
yearns in the desperateness of her need but whom she cannot
distinguish from the hated mother imago deemed to be responsi-
ble for her distress). Of the latter, the one at the other end of the
"Old barnacled umbilicus, Atlantic cable" in the poem called
"Medusa," she writes: "I shall take no bite of your body," and
concludes:

> Off, off, eely tentacle!
>
> There is nothing between us.

But "Poppies in July" articulates an unresolvable ambivalence in
the form of infinite yearning and unconquerable rage. Much of
the poem's power derives from the body language that bridges
the surface meaning of longing for death with the more profound
coordinates of this longing. The images of touching and tactile
pain (burning) combine with the speaker's inability to touch, or
make contact with, the flicker and the fumes, thus expressing

Sylvia Plath's yearning to make contact with this unreachable mother. Through a series of abrupt associational leaps and bounds, she links images of punishment, harm, absence of feeling, exhaustion, petals "wrinkly and clear red, like the skin of a mouth" to further images of a bloodied mouth and bloodied skirts and then to the masochistic wish:

> If my mouth could marry a hurt like that!

That wish, if magically fulfilled, would bring the colorless sleep of death. In what might be called the psychotic calculus of Plath's undifferentiated emotions, the bloody skirts of the poppies become the burning skin of a bloodied mouth to be kissed. This is mother's mouth, and the kiss is the kiss of death. What on the surface of the poem appear to be images of sexual perversity really represent images of symbiotic fusion, or boundarylessness, and the poem leads, finally, to the boundaryless state of the last six words of the poem: "Dulling and stilling./But colourless. Colourless."

While I am in the process of reading this poem, the mouth imagery reminds me of similar images elsewhere, such as the smothering, oxygen-gulping mouths of the flowers in "Tulips": "They are opening like the mouth of some great African cat." I think also of the "Black sweet blood mouthfuls" of the pain-giving "Nigger-eye/Berries" of the briars in "Ariel." Especially I think in this connection of the "perfected" death of the woman in "Edge" who has folded the bodies of her two dead children

> . . . back into her body as petals
> Of a rose close when the garden
>
> Stiffens and odours bleed
> From the sweet, deep throats of the night flower.

Plath projectively identifies with her own mother in "Edge," reversing the process of birth by returning her children (and thus herself) to the place from which she came, the child begotten to the place begot. The reunion must be a bodily one. As Bollas and Schwartz say, "Just as the father is perceived as cannibalistic, the vampire of 'Daddy', so the mother imago shares Plath's voracious obsession with the mouth as the psychic representative of the whole person."[21] They see this theme as reflecting a psychotic wish to re-enter the mother's mouth-womb, as Esther Greenwood does symbolically in *The Bell Jar*: "The breezeway had been added to the house after the cellar was dug, and built out over this secret, earth-bottomed crevice. A few old, rotting fireplace logs blocked the hole mouth. I shoved them back a bit. . . . It took me a good while to heft my body into the gap, but at last, after many tries, I managed it, and crouched at the mouth of the darkness, like a troll."[22]

The poetry of Sylvia Plath suggests that the more profound the regressional dynamics of a work of art, the more likely we will encounter relatively pure somatic equivalents of emotion. Much of the power of her work to touch us to the quick lies in the way her body imagery generates an almost cancerous primary-process mentation in the reader. This power would not exist, I believe, if Sylvia Plath had not drawn so heavily on the wellsprings of her own primary process.

A few words in this anatomy need to be reserved for what may be referred to, for lack of a better term, as genital poetry. Within the limits of this rubric I mean to include not just lines referring directly to the genitalia, like Mercutio's "The bawdy hand of the dial is now upon the prick of noon" or like the sly disquisition on orgasmic timing by the wit in "The Rape of the Lock" who says to Belinda,

> Nor think to die dejects my lofty mind:
> All that I dread is leaving you behind!
> Rather than so, ah, let me still survive,
> And burn in Cupid's flames—but burn alive.

By the phrase "genital poetry" I mean to include all work operating primarily on the level of adult, heterosexual, overt, genital sexuality. Earlier stages of psychosexual development, even if in evidence, are not the main level of interest. Though there are complications—in fact, there is no such thing as a libidinal level uncontaminated by any other—a poem like Shakespeare's "Venus and Adonis" would fall into this category, as would much of a play

21. Ibid., p. 163.
22. Sylvia Plath, *The Bell Jar* (New York: Harper and Row, 1971), pp. 190-91.

like *Romeo and Juliet*. Sometimes much of a poet's canon falls
into the category of genital poetry—John Donne's, for one. He
argues directly for what psychoanalysis calls genital primacy in
"Love's Progress." "Perfection is in unitie," he says; "preferr
/ One woman first, and then one thing in her." Cupid is really a
god of the underworld. "Men to such Gods, their sacrificing
Coles / Did not in Altar's lay, but pits and holes."

The question to be raised about all such poetry has to do with
the dynamics of our response to it. Clearly it has appeal. Clearly
conscious sexual metaphors can mobilize conscious primary process mentation—spontaneous mental pictures of the body, for
example. It is also probable that overt sexual imagery mobilizes a
good deal of the primary process that remains dynamically unconscious. What may not be clear is that such poetic language
probably does not normally generate as much psychosexual tension as does imagery more covert in its appeal. It is impossible to
take measurements in such matters. Or if it is not impossible, at
least no important critical work has been done along the lines of
testing galvanic skin response.

Still water runs deep. If overt sexual imagery stirs us *more
readily but less profoundly,* as I speculate, this circumstance has
some import for contemporary poetry. Wallace Stevens mentions
the problem in "The Noble Rider and the Sound of Words" when
he says, "Boileau's remark that Descartes had cut poetry's throat
is a remark that could have been made respecting a great many
people during the last hundred years, and of no one more aptly
than Freud."[23] I. A. Richards raises much the same question in
Science and Poetry: "Consider the probable effects upon love
poetry in the near future of the kind of enquiry into basic human
constitution exemplified by psychoanalysis."[24] One effect of living in a post-Freudian era is that besides encountering a lot of
Freudian posts and postholes, we often find writers dispensing
with symbolism altogether at the genital level.

Evidence looms. Here is an example of the body as landscape
in Gary Snyder's "Beneath My Hand and Eye the Distant Hills,
Your Body." It begins,

23. In *The Language of Poetry*, ed. Allen Tate (New York: Russell and Russell,
1960), p. 103.

24. I. A. Richards, *Science and Poetry* (London: Kegan Paul, Trench, Trubner &
Co., 1926), p. 64.

> What my hand follows on your body
> Is the line. A stream of love
>   of heat, of light, what my
> eye lascivious
>   licks
> over, watching
> far snow-dappled Unitah mountains
> Is that stream,
> Of power.   what my
>   hand curves over, following the line,
>   "hip" and "groin."

Such poetry has immediacy of appeal. The licking eye is poetic
enough. Yet the eye ends up doing what eyes do: they watch.
Hands do what hands do: they caress. And snow-dappled or otherwise, mammalian mountains are no far cry from rosy cheeks. The
metaphors shoot slack. Similarly, there is even less psychosexual
tension in this recent verse by Karen Waring:

> Why should the poem
> Tell
> How you felt inside
> Me,
> Banging stars
> Into my womb.

Why, asks the poetess, should her words describe the way

> You came in pain
> The way you
> Backed out
> All shining
> And covered with tears?

The poem answers its own question by demonstrating the dubi-
ousness of trying to get words to tell such things, at least to try to
articulate them in so inarticulate a way through the medium of
slang, dead metaphor, and literalism. Despite the apparent sin-
cerity of feeling in the experience described, this kind of work
tempts one to say that Freud was not so cruel as to cut Poetry's
throat; he merely tied off her tubes.

These days, to use the current body cliché, poets let it all hang
out. Sometimes this strategy, rightly used, works well—as in
Anne Sexton's sardonic complaint, "The Ballad of the Lonely
Masturbator." It begins,

The end of the affair is always death.
She's my workshop. Slippery eye,
out of the tribe of myself my breath
finds you gone. I horrify
those who stand by. I am fed.
At night, alone, I marry the bed.

And the last stanza reads,

The boys and girls are one tonight.
They unbutton blouses. They unzip flies.
They take off shoes. They turn off the light.
The glimmering creatures are full of lies.
They are eating each other. They are overfed.
At night, alone, I marry the bed.

Contemporary verse is full of sexuality as direct as this, not to mention movies and other media. When tempered with irony, as in "The Ballad of the Lonely Masturbator," or otherwise enhanced, what I have been calling genital poetry leaves the reader some room for imaginative freedom, as in these delightful lines by Theodore Roethke:

I knew a woman, lovely in her bones,
When small birds sighed, she would sigh back at them;
Ah, when she moved, she moved more ways than one:
The shapes a bright container can contain!

The poet wishing to arouse his reader to the fullest will couch his feelings in the language of the body in ways that will allow the reader to occupy a relatively large cultural and psychological space instead of pinning him to the mat with the limitations of a sweaty literalism of the body. The reason is not because overt sexual imagery, especially genital imagery, will fail to mobilize the primary process. It will do so, abundantly, in the same way obscene language and visual pornography do. What it will not do is generate very much of what I call modal ambiguity. Hence it will not provide the kind of psychological space the reader's imagination needs for the fullest, freest, most satisfying kind of mental play, the kind of playspace D. W. Winnicott regards as the space of "transitional phenomena," which is in turn, he says, the prototype of cultural space. He assumes that people never complete the task of reality-acceptance: "No human being is free from the strain of relating inner and outer reality. . . . Relief

from this strain is provided by an intermediate area of experience
. . . which is not challenged (arts, religion, etc.). This intermediate
area is in direct continuity with the play area of the small child
who is 'lost' in play."[25] Artspace is therefore part of the playspace
of grown-up children.

It may now be asked how metaphor serves to generate an
expanded boundary or potential space in the mind of the reader.
This process can be understood more fully in terms of the concept
of *analytic space* in psychoanalytic psychotherapy. In discussing
apparent shifts in styles of being a patient and ways of handling
the transference, André Green stresses the concept of absence.[26]
He refers to the desirability of the analyst helping borderline
patients to develop a dimension of absence that will serve as
potential space in the analysis. Green suggests that the borderline
patient cannot constitute the absence of the object. "The object
. . . is always intrusively present, permanently occupying the
personal psychic space. . . . Never being absent, it cannot be
thought." These patients have trouble with what Green refers to
as symbolization. They equate but do not form symbols. In other
words, Green is talking about what can be called pre-symbolic
mentation, such as occurs in the psychotic's use of unlabelled
metaphor. Green is also talking about what amounts to the
inability of some people to distinguish between their own emotional or psychic space and the personal space of important
Others.

In contrast to such patients, an artist like Sylvia Plath excels in
symbolization. She operates in and around the same boundaries
as the borderline patient, yet she has an exceptional capacity to
create absence in the mind of the reader and at the same time to
fill that absence with the presence of the missing *symbolic* object.
How? She does it through the transference. I do not of course
refer to the analytic concept of transference but to the transference, or transfer, inherent in every metaphor. The transfer
creates the absence, the object-relational vacuum which the other
meanings of the image rush to fill in. Figures of speech embody

25. D. W. Winnicott, *Playing and Reality* (New York: Basic Books, 1971), pp. 13
and 95-103. See also Murray Schwartz, "Where is Literature?" *College English 36*
(March, 1975): 756-65.

26. André Green, "The Analyst, Symbolization and Absence in the Analytic
Setting," *Int. J. Psycho-Anal.* 56 (1975): 1-22.

the figure of the lost object. Freud sees the schizophrenic's use of words as an attempt to regain the lost object.[27] What he claims for schizophrenics holds for all of us. The restitution of lost objects occurs by virtue of the restitution of lost images the poet makes in metaphor.

Masud Khan speaks about the need for special efforts to develop the analytic space with certain patients by comparing what happens in classical psychoanalysis to cases with borderline patients who do not conform to the traditional assumptions about treatability in analysis: "In the classical analytic space we rely upon language to do all this," he says, referring to the way Marion Milner is able to utilize, in the case of Susan, the pictorial space of the drawings for processes which are not becoming actualized in the therapeutic space through verbalization. "Furthermore," continues Khan, "we create a void and an absence from our presence to create that space of illusion where the patient can use symbolic discourse."[28] In short, the difficult, borderline type of patient Green and Khan are discussing does not have the resources to participate fully in the symbolic or metaphoric processes of therapy, at least not to begin with and not without special help, whereas the classic neurotic patient is from the very beginning able to use a language of symbolic discourse comparable to that articulated by the poet and expropriated by the responding reader. What seems to me to be of inestimable importance is that one of the major ways the writer has of creating this void or absence that in turn creates the space of illusion where the reader can enter into literature's symbolic discourse lies in the way the artist exploits the paradoxical potential metaphor has for representing a present absence.

27. "The Unconscious," *Std. Ed.*, XIV, pp. 203-204.
28. M. Masud R. Khan, "The Role of Illusion in the Analytic Space and Process," in *The Privacy of the Self* (New York: International Universities Press, 1974), p. 266.

4

A Gathering of Roses

∽∾∽∾∽∾∽∾∽∾∽∾∽∾∽∾∽∾∽∾∽∾∽∾∽∾∽∾∽

> All night by the rose, rose—
> All night by the rose I lay;
> Dared I not the rose steal,
> And yet I bore the flower away.
> —Anon.

T. S. Eliot illustrates the splitting-up of the poet's intellectual and emotional capacities by an odd simile as he discusses the "dissociation of sensibility" alleged to have set in during the seventeenth century.[1] As he compares the metaphysical poets to Tennyson and Browning he says that the latter "are poets, and they think; but they do not feel their thought as immediately as the odour of a rose." While the simile makes a kind of sense, it remains a rather puzzling comparison for the rapidity and directness of the conjunction of feeling and thought. How can a thought be felt? And why does Eliot reach for a rose at this explanatory moment?

---

1. T. S. Eliot, "The Metaphysical Poets," in *Selected Essays* (New York: Harcourt, Brace, 1950), pp. 214-50. For an account placing Eliot's concept of dissociated sensibility in the context of literary history and modern criticism, see Frank Kermode, *The Romantic Image* (New York: Vintage, 1964), pp. 138-61. For an excellent general survey of the literary history of roses, including Eliot's handling of rose symbolism, see Barbara Seward's *The Symbolic Rose* (New York: Columbia University Press, 1960).

Apparently he takes his cue from a twelve-line passage he has just been quoting from Tennyson, a passage describing a wife as "wearing the rose of womanhood." Though Eliot does not pause to discuss this image, he subsequently appropriates it, or part of it, almost as an afterthought. The limits of Tennyson's rose metaphor are vague:

> The prudent partner of his blood
> Leaned on him, faithful, gentle, good,
> Wearing the rose of womanhood.

Tennyson's image could be one of rose-colored clothing or a rose-like complexion, or an actual rose adorning the wife's hat or hair as an emblem of female beauty. Since husband and wife walk with their daughter ("The little maiden walked demure, / Pacing with downward eyelids pure"), the poem also presents a veiled contrast between the virginal girl and her sexually mature mother. Be that as it may, the rose metaphor feels conventional here. It is not, in any case, a trope to strain a brain, whereas Eliot creates an image that forces the reader to think when he says some poets do not feel their thought with the immediacy of the odor of a rose. Eliot's imaginative image for felt thought constitutes his own version of what he calls Chapman's "direct sensuous apprehension of thought."

Perhaps one reason why Eliot reached for a rose at this moment is that this particular flower enjoys special poetic status. Out of his great sense of literary tradition, Eliot chose the rose to bridge the gap between thought and feeling because he knew the manifold ways roses can link passion with idealism, the concrete with the abstract, the profane with the sacred. In all probability the poet in Eliot delighted in accepting the challenge of doing something new with a metaphor so widely used yet so intrinsically poetic that it might be called an ur-metaphor.

The discussion of this ur-metaphor to follow attempts to assess the potential range of thought and feeling in metaphoric beds of roses by examining a number of more or less unrelated contexts to discover what associations such images may have in common. This procedure violates the psychoanalytic rule that interpretation of symbols must follow the lead of the individual's associations, which in the case of literature amounts to responding to the contextual cues reflecting the personal associations a writer incorporates in a given work. Here lies the difference between reading the relatively idiosyncratic, individual dreams of an analysand and reading the trans-individual dreams contained in the fantasies of literature. It would be sheer dogmatism to believe all unconscious literary symbolism *sui generis,* dictated solely by the psychic whim of a particular author's anomalous trains of association. Such a view would allow for agreed-upon meanings of sign and symbol at the secondary-process level of conscious communication but treat the primary process as a virtual chaos—a demonstrable error. On the contrary, poets deserving of the name can communicate unerringly through the primary process. They may write out of private conflict, but their words are for public consumption.

As we consider this multitude of blossoms—seeking to know what burden a rose can bear—three issues might be kept in mind: the range of meaning and emotion a single basic image can bring into focus in a given context, the range of meaning and emotion such an image may reflect in a variety of contexts, and the relative stability of meaning that perseveres throughout a variety of contexts. The overall issue might be called the problem of the limits of context. Is the potential context of a poetic image limited to the poem in which it occurs, the canon or individual mind of the author, the centuries-spanning mind of conscious literary tradition, or the more inclusive, culture-spanning associations of the human mind itself as they become embodied in the linguistic and cultural heritage forming, in turn, part of the ontogenetic associational ecology of the individual reader of the poem?

Some recent work in the theory of response to literature makes rather imperialistic claims on behalf of the notion that the mind of the reader of the poem is the context of the poem. Much as beauty must be in the eye of the beholder, in this view so must the poem be what the reader makes of it. For all practical purposes, the poem is *in* the reader rather than *on* the page or *from* the writer.[2] No extensive examination of the question of the location of information in the total literary process will be forthcoming here, but for the moment I will at least say, for the record, that

2. See Norman N. Holland, *Poems in Persons* (New York: Norton, 1973) and *5 Readers Reading* (New Haven: Yale University Press, 1975).

the personal identity of the reader who necessarily shapes the text to some extent as he reads cannot be regarded as somehow liberated from the constraints upon interpretation inhering in the text of the poem. The reader's identity may be regarded as one of a number of "competing" contexts within which the poem is read. Among these contexts I would include the mind of the author as it is reflected in his other work and the collective experience of the culture within which the poem emerges.

This chapter anticipates a quite different range of demonstrations I plan to make in subsequent work about the capaciousness of metaphor as a vessel of thought and emotion. The approaches differ significantly. The subsequent studies will dwell on what I call the microdramatic aspects of metaphor by focusing on the plenitude of more or less unique metaphors in the fullness of their related verbal contexts where such contexts amount in scope to a poem the length of a Shakespearean play or, in the case of a lyric poet, to the extra-textual context of his complete literary production. This chapter suggests the amplitude of a single traditional metaphor by looking at a large number of its occurrences in a wide variety of contexts.

The tribute to feminine beauty constitutes one of the most familiar varieties of poetic rose. It occurs in Robert Burns's "O, my luve is like a red, red rose,/That's newly sprung in June." It appears in Edmund Waller's

> Go, lovely Rose—
> Tell her that wastes her time and me
>   That now she knows,
> When I resemble her to thee,
> How sweet and fair she seems to be.

If the range of these rose images itself is somewhat limited and conventional, as in the garden variety of lips "like rosebuds filled with snow" in Thomas Campion's "There is a Garden in Her Face," these poets nevertheless succeed in delighting readers by their nimble artifice in marshalling familiar themes, rhymes, and rhythms in new combinations. Another rosy tribute can be found in these lines of Richard Lovelace:

> See! rosy in her bower,
> Her floor is all this flower;
>   Her bed a rosy nest
>   By a bed of roses pressed.
>
> But early as she dresses,
> Why fly you her bright tresses?
>   Ah! I have found, I fear—
>   Because her cheeks are near.

Among the rarest of blooms in this general variety are those of Robert Herrick's lovely, witty "How Roses Came Red":

> Roses at first were white,
>   Till they could not agree
> Whether my Sappho's breast
>   Or they more white should be
>
> But being vanquished quite,
>   A blush their cheeks bespread;
> Since which, believe the rest,
>   The roses first came red.

For the most part, all such rose imagery is delicate of growth. The associations in the foreground have to do with color, fragrance, texture, and related attributes of feminine allure. The ranker growth of genital associations lies so far in the background as to be almost invisible, though a host of subsidiary metaphors like "bower," "rosy *nest,*" and "bed" lead our minds in that direction. Body images, like "dresses," "tresses," "cheek," "blush," and "breast," tend to mobilize erotic feeling, whether we are conscious of it or not. The process is essentially that of "contamination" of a beneficial, controlled, and largely invisible sort. It cannot be avoided where body images abound. Wordsworth can say,

> The Rainbow comes and goes,
> And lovely is the Rose,

and manage to limit our attention to a fairly disembodied beauty, but the minute a woman enters the scene it is impossible (in the full thematic context of *As You Like It*) to read Orlando's silly couplet,

> He that sweetest rose will find
> Must find love's prick and Rosalind,

without having the metaphors themselves begin to couple in our minds.

The compost of tradition nurtures many of the conscious associations cultivated in the poet's rose garden. Exactly because these images are so conventional, the greatest art lies in the variety achieved with iconography standard in substance but fresh in treatment. But the poet's intuitive reliance on sexual overtones must be the most vital source of emotive power, with freshness of treatment functioning primarily as an aesthetic bribe—as in this cluster of passages from Shakespeare.

> Fair ladies masked are roses in their bud.
> Dismasked, their damask sweet commixture shown,
> Are angels vailing clouds, or roses blown.
>
> *[Love's Labour's Lost]*

The duke in *Twelfth Night* says,

> For women are as roses, whose fair flower
> Being once displayed, doth fall that very hour.

Viola wittily responds,

> And so they are. Alas, that they are so—
> To die, even when they to perfection grow!

Confusion of the seasons gets described this way in *Midsummer Night's Dream*:

> Hoary-headed frosts
> Fall in the fresh lap of the crimson rose.

No reader of Shakespeare can deal with "fresh lap" and "crimson rose" in one line—with or without a verb like "fall"—and fail to apprehend a monstrous mismating of the seasons here. Genital overtones "contaminate" such an image in a functional way, giving it depth and resonance, as also happens in a more subtle way in the other passages just quoted.

Since it becomes increasingly difficult to avert our eyes from what is going on in the bushes, the time has come to stare at some of the more frankly genital blooms. Matthew Prior gives us a tried maid named Rose in "A True Maid":

> No, no, for my Virginity,
> When I lose that, says ROSE, I'll dye:
> Behind the Elmes, last Night, cry'd DICK
> ROSE, were You not extreamly Sick?

Shelley includes an image of defloration at once literal and figurative in "To a Skylark":

> Like a rose embowered
> In its own green leaves,
> By warm winds deflowered,
> Till the scent it gives
> Makes faint with too much sweet those heavy-wingèd thieves.

It is Spenser, in the "Bowre of Blisse" episode of the *Faerie Queene*, who provides us with one of the most memorable passages:

> Ah see the Virgin Rose, how sweetly shee
> Doth first peepe forth with bashful modestee
> That fairer seemes, the lesse ye see her may
> Lo see soone after, how more bold and free
> Her barèd bosome she doth broad display:
> Loe see soone after, how she fades, and falles away.

Spenser articulates the classic theme of *carpe diem* with perfect directness and simplicity in the subsequent stanza:

> Gather therefore the Rose, whilest yet is prime
> For soone comes age, that will her pride deflowre
> Gather the Rose of love, whilest yet is time,
> Whilest loving thou mayst lovèd be with equall crime.

The most elaborate treatment of the rose in all literature appears in Guillaume de Lorris' *Romance of the Rose*, a medieval allegory beginning with the God of Love shooting an arrow (Beauty) through the eye of Dreamer, and into his heart when he sees the rose more pleasing than any other.

It would be painting an inch thick to unveil more roses of this kind. Instead I will turn from the sublime to what may look like the ridiculous: the hybrid roses of Gertrude Stein. She declares her own rosehood in a poem called "I am a Rose":

I am Rose my eyes are blue
I am Rose and who are you
I am Rose and when I sing
I am Rose like anything

The most famous passage ever written by this blushing rose is "A rose is a rose is a rose is a rose." Stein's iteration appears to insist that a rose is, after all, only a rose and hence literal. At the same time—in a not necessarily contradictory way—the triumphant tautology of the rose proclaims the figurativeness of the redundancy itself, making way for the possibility of the presence in the passage of yearning and ecstasy and even perhaps a kind of defiant exclusiveness. That some such feelings are expressed is evident from the gloss Gertrude Stein provides for this passage in an essay in which she distinguishes prose from poetry by insisting that, unlike prose, poetry is based on vocabulary, especially the noun.[3] Poetry is "a vocabulary entirely based on the noun . . . Poetry is concerned with using with abusing, with losing with wanting, with denying with avoiding with adoring with replacing the noun," she says. That is what poetry does and nothing but that. "Poetry is doing nothing but using losing refusing and pleasing and betraying and caressing nouns." And then she adds,

> That is what poetry does, that is what poetry has to do no matter what kind of poetry it is. And there are a great many kinds of poetry.
> When I said.
> A rose is a rose is a rose is a rose.
> And then later made that into a ring I made poetry and what did I do I caressed completely caressed and addressed a noun.
> Now let us think of poetry any poetry all poetry and let us see if this is not so.

If anything that Gertrude Stein ever said made sense, this definition of poetry does, but of more immediate concern here is what she tell us about the rose more pleasing than any other, and what it means to her, and why she made a straight line into a ring, and why she—like Eliot—reached for a rose at this explanatory moment.

Given the relative stability of the usual associations linked with

---

3. Gertrude Stein, "Poetry and Grammar," in *Lectures in America* (New York: Random House, 1935), pp. 209-46; quotations from p. 231.

roses in the examples thus far, it may cause surprise to consider that one variation of the rose metaphor involves its application to males in the form of a fairly generalized, conventional symbol of youthful perfection. Shakespeare speaks of "beauty's rose" in this sense in "Sonnet #1," and Ophelia speaks of Hamlet in a comparable way:

> Oh, what a noble mind is here o'erthrown!
> The courtier's, soldier's, eye, tongue, sword—
> The expectancy and rose of the fair state,
> The glass of fashion and the mold of form.

In *The Spanish Tragedy* Hieronimo addresses these impassioned words of grief to the corpse of his son:

> Sweet lovely rose, ill pluck'd before thy time,
> Fair, worthy son, not conquer'd, but betray'd,
> I'll kiss thee now, for words with tears are stay'd.

In Melville's *Billy Budd* the protagonist looks younger than he is "owing to a lingering adolescent expression in the as yet smooth face all but feminine in purity in natural complexion but where, thanks to his seagoing, the lily was quite suppressed and the rose had some ado visibly to flush through the tan." Even Billy's surname has floral implications, and he is referred to, at one point, as "the flower" of the king's flock. Part of the originality of these otherwise conventional rose images may lie in the transfer of the metaphoric transfer to an unexpected yet not totally alien gestalt.

Another significant variation on the usual range of meaning occurs when rose imagery either takes on the overtones of anality or comes into close associational contact, in the constricted space of a particular context, with other images bearing anality in their wake. Keats's Endymion encounters the dream-maiden "sweet as a muskrose" on new-made hay early in Book IV, but when he utters some gloomy thoughts the lady warns him not to spoil his chances by spoiling her mood:

> Speak not of grief, young stranger, or cold snails
> will slime the rose to night.

While the seminal implications of "slime" cannot be avoided, neither can the nymph's foul image fairly avoid the anal connotations of dirtiness adhering to this term. The slimy snail on the rose illustrates how "good" genital imagery can be contaminated by "bad" anal inflections in a manner guaranteed to produce considerable endopsychic tension. If perspiration and body odor are psychologically anal in value—as this nation's compulsive annual consumption of so many tons of antiperspirants would seem to indicate—then the lines at the beginning of Donne's anti-Petrarchan "Elegie VIII" ("The Comparison") provide an example of foul-smelling roses:

> As the sweet sweat of Roses in a Still,
> As that which from chaf'd muskats pores doth trill,
> As the Almighty Balme of th' early East,
> Such are the sweat drops of my Mistris breast

More strange, because serious, is Crashaw's comparable image of the weeping Mary Magdalene:

> Such tears the suff'ring rose that's vexed
> With ungentle flames does shed,
> Sweating in a too warm bed.

While anality may be of oblique significance in this catachresis, anality cannot be irrelevant or insignificant, though it may be unconscious, in William Faulkner's tribute to an intransigeant lady in the story called "A Rose for Emily." One is tempted to say that no rose, by any other name, could well smell worse. Emily, a rose of southern womanhood, secretes the decaying corpse of her poisoned lover in the rose-colored bedroom of the old family house in grotesque unconscious parody of the way she retained her father's precious body after his death until it began to smell— a parody, in turn, of Emily's anal-retentive model for holding on by holding in.[4]

In most contexts the odor of a rose may be thought of as involving sublimation of olfactory ugliness into scented beauty. This kind of sensuous transaction occurs in Shelley's rose de-flowered by warm winds "Till the scent it gives / Makes faint with too much sweet those heavy-wingéd thieves." In the same passage there appears the almost equally characteristic attribu-tion of sweetness to the odor, the direct reference being to the

4. The complex anality of this story has been assessed by Norman N. Holland in "Fantasy and Defense in Faulkner's 'A Rose for Emily'," *Hartford Studies in Literature* IV (1972): 1-35.

honey-making "thieves." When odors are described as sweet in such passages, there will often occur a conventional allusion to the electuary called "sugar of roses," as in the third stanza of Herbert's "Vertue":

> Sweet spring, full of sweet dayes and roses,
> A box where sweets compacted lie:
> My musick shows ye have your closes,
> And all must die.

Underlying the immediate orality of most such "roses are red . . . sugar is sweet" configurations is the ultimate orality of the idealized, abstracted love object—the other as nurturing other. Food is love and love is food. It becomes impossible, as Norman O. Brown says in *Love's Body*, to make any complete, categorical separation of coital and oral sexuality.

While there are sometimes "Serpents in red roses hissing," as in Keats's "A Song of Opposites," roses themselves are without phallic attributes, as might be expected. Thorns can be phallic but not the blossoms. In fact, when Keats writes in his sonnet on fame, "It is as if the rose should pluck herself," this masturbatory image churns up negative affect by paralleling the conscious awareness that "roses do not, in nature, pluck themselves" with the preconscious attribution of a projective activity to a passive-receptive organ.

What then, with all these primary-process nodes of meaning and feeling twangling in our Caliban ears, are we to do with a conventional iconography depicting Christ as a rose, as in the imagery of Crashaw's "Hymn for New Year's Day"? This day is the anniversary of the circumcision of the Lord, and the blood imagery refers to this rite of passage and foreshadows the blood of the passion. The first verse reads,

> Rise, thou best and brightest morning!
> Rosy with a double Red:
> With thine own blush thy cheeks adorning
> And the dear drops this day were shed.

And the third verse:

> Of all the fair-cheek't flowrs that fill thee
> None so fair thy bosom strowes,
> As this modest maiden lilly
> Our sins have sham'd into a rose.

Or one might ask how Christ becomes the rose of Sharon. While this is not the place to attempt to trace by what charmed routes the language of erotic passion comes to be used for expressing spiritual passion, it may be permissible to take it for granted that this kind of speaking in tongues does regularly take place. Instead of attempting such an enquiry here, it would be better to dwell for a moment on some of the pertinent associations with roses which have become crystallized over the course of centuries into a traditional iconography transmissible from poet to poet and poet to reader.

The discussion of this iconography draws freely upon the account rendered by Don Cameron Allen in his own excellent study of the poem about to be explored further: George Herbert's "The Rose."[5] There are actually three traditions: secular, pagan, and Christian. Most of the secular elements have already been mentioned. Roses are associated with transitory loveliness, youth, virginity, the female genitals, and death. Pagan associations can almost be lumped with the secular ones. Roses make a chaplet for Venus, a crown for Bacchus, and a wreath for the sickle of Chronos. Writing in the Christian tradition, St. Ambrose says—I am quoting Allen—"that the rose, once it has taken thorns, is the symbol of man surrounded by briars of pricking care and sharp desire." Some of the iconography of the *Divine Comedy* epitomizes elements of the Christian tradition of roses: "The Mother of God is the rose without a thorn." "The closed garden, says Dante, on which the light of Christ shone, brought forth the rose in which the Divine Word is made flesh: 'Quivi è la rosa in che il Verbo Divino / Carne si fece.' " Following these traditions in "Ash Wednesday," T. S. Eliot presents both Mary and her Son in rose imagery:

> Lady of silences
> Calm and distressed
> Torn and most whole
> Rose of memory
> Rose of forgetfulness
> Exhausted and life-giving
> Worried reposeful
> The single Rose

5. Don Cameron Allen, *Image and Meaning: Metaphoric Traditions in Renaissance Poetry* (Baltimore: Johns Hopkins Press, 1960), chapter 4, pp. 67-79.

> Is now the Garden
> Where all loves end

The sacred rose becomes an established symbol for Mary, Christ, Christianity, and spiritual love.

Many of these traditional meanings, including secular ones, combine in Herbert's poem, though the sexual implications are very indirect. More immediately confronting the reader's attention is the moral significance of the work. Here, in the first four stanzas, the speaker declines the sweet deceits of worldliness and offers, as a substitute, the "gentle rose" of Christianity:

> Presse me not to take more pleasure
>   In this world of sugred lies,
> And to use a larger measure
>   Than my strict, yet welcome size.
>
> First, there is no pleasure here:
>   Colour'd griefs indeed there are,
> Blushing woes, that look as cleare
>   As if they could beautie spare.
>
> Of if such deceits there be,
>   Such delights I meant to say;
> There are no such things to me
>   Who have pass'd my right away.
>
> But I will not much oppose
>   Unto what you now advise:
> Only take this gentle rose,
>   And therein my answer lies.

Allen thinks these lines are addressed to a man of the world. They may also be thought of as an apostrophe to a rose blossom symbolizing the world's delights—or the lines might even be addressed to a lovely woman, herself a rose of womanhood. There are at least two speakers: Herbert and the rose of Christianity. Allen suggests that Christ in person may be thought of as delivering the gentle lecture making up the latter half of the poem:

> What is fairer than a rose?
>   What is sweeter? yet it purgeth.
> Purgings enmitie disclose,
>   Enmities forebearance urgeth.
>
> If then all that worldlings prize
>   Be contracted to a rose;

> Sweetly there indeed it lies,
> But it biteth in the close.
>
> So this flower doth judge and sentence
> Worldly joyes to be a scourge:
> For they all produce repentance,
> And repentance is a purge.
>
> But I health, not physick choose:
> Only though I you oppose,
> Say that fairly I refuse,
> For my answer is a rose.

So much thought and feeling lie compacted in these lines that I should like to add to what Allen says about them, especially since he avoids the grosser features. He locates the sexual elements in the iconographic tradition rather than in the poem itself, and he shuns elaboration of the medicinal theme which, from a psychoanalytic perspective, is inescapably anal and ineluctably involved in the astonishing amount of imagistic tension generated by this quiet poem.

The formal measuredness and the calm, assured tone of the work are deceptive. Hidden beneath the surface beauty of "The Rose" lie some thorny oppositions. In painful contrast to the temperate, "gentle" rose of Christianity is the rose that purges and scourges. Analogous to sugar-of-roses used as a purgative is the sweetness of sin—the fleshes exercise—represented as leading to an oral retching or an anal discharge or a spiritual anguish. So "this flower" judges and sentences "Worldly joyes to be a scourge." Acceptance of Christianity, since it produces repentance, also purges—the ironic reverse of this thought being that Christianity gives the condition of grace opposite to the sickness that is worldliness ("But I health, not physick choose"). Another source of cognitive dissonance in the poem is the thought that "Purgings enmitie disclose," so that Christian forbearance and temperance are placed in opposition to rosy indulgence in the "deceits" admitted to be "delights" in the third stanza.

A number of bitter words, like "enmitie," "purge," "scourge," "judge," and "sentence," prevent the careful reader of this poem from finding anything cloying in its sweetnesses. Among these severe words is "biteth." All that wordlings prize is contracted in a rose: "Sweetly there indeed it lies,/But it biteth in the close." Is this biting an oral-sadistic one? While the amount of orality in the poem permits this possibility, the grosser images of anal catharsis suggest a pain-giving sphincteral contraction caused by the purgative. Allen's suggestion, reasonable enough, is that "close" refers to a thorny rose "biting" the hand that grasps the plant stem. But we have already seen Herbert employ "close" in the musical sense in "Vertue": "My music shows ye have your closes,/And all must die." While "close" does not necessarily include the musical sense in "The Rose," the meanings surrounding that term in "Vertue" suggest that "close" in "The Rose" can refer to an eschatological ending, to the end of individual life, to orgasmic death, to a genital contraction or closing, to the already mentioned sphincteral closure, and to the anal analogue of orgasm: catharsis.

A biting rose looks ominous. If genital, the image becomes another variation on the familiar theme of the vagina dentata. To say so does not attribute anything pathological to Herbert's mind, or the reader's, but only insists the poem invites this reading. What Shakespeare says is that "The expense of spirit in a waste of shame/Is lust in action." What Herbert does is to put teeth into the idea that lust in action eventuates in painful retribution and one ought therefore to choose the gentler rose of Christianity. By inflaming genital imagery with the colitus of a harsh, negatively toned anality, Herbert reinforces the anal-erotic dimension of the moral fervor of the poem. This dimension centers around the themes of *power* (the gentle rose versus the scourge), *value* ("all that worldlings prize"), the *anal-sadistic* theme (reflected in the sphincteral bite and the power of the retribution), the *masochistic* theme of submission to God's rule, the theme of *reward* for Christian submission, the theme of the *beauty* of Christianity, the *active-passive* dichotomy (as in "Presse me not to take more pleasure"), and in the general theme of *control* (moral control of impulse analogous to sphincteral control) enhanced by the great formal control exercised over the strenuous dialectic of thought and emotion in the poem. Since the rose symbolizes a great range of "higher" and "lower" modalities of love, it seems reasonable to suppose this lyric produces endopsychic tension commensurate with the gravity of its subject by setting up a series of oppositions between conscious, conventional meanings and unconscious, psychosexual "affective correlatives" of the imagery.

Ernst Kris and Abraham Kaplan contend that in the case of ambiguous language, as opposed to the rigorously limited meaning of a code or sign language, "one cannot speak . . . of *the* meaning of any symbol, but can only specify its range of responses and the clusters into which these tend to be grouped."[6] The rose imagery we have been considering reveals a full spectrum of the range of meanings possible within the framework of modal ambiguity. To be specific, this imagery shows a wide range of meaning in the more codified secondary-process mode where a rose may be Christian, pagan; sacred, profane; ideal, real; male, female; sensual or merely sensuous; a symbol of sexual innocence (especially in the form of a bud) or its opposite, experience; and may bring to mind ideas like beauty and ephemerality. The rose reflects a comparable range of meaning within the primary-process mode. Associative constellations can include that which is oral-nourishing, oral-sadistic; anal-retentive, anal-expulsive; sadistic, masochistic; phallic—if we include the thorns; and almost everything that pertains to genitality, including related material like defloration and the blood associated with that act. It does not of course follow that all of the sexual symbolism moves in one direction, that is, that all nonsexual imagery and ideation in Herbert's "The Rose" symbolizes something sexual or vice versa. The rose is just as sacred as it is profane in this work by a poet so much given to the direct sensuous apprehension of thought that he symbolizes what he regards as the deceitful sweets and painful ephemerality of "worldly joyes" by a rose and in the same creative breath represents the beauty of Christian idealism by this emblem.

There is no need to be rigid about variety. The rose metaphors we have examined exhibit a remarkable stability of thought and feeling—so much so that it becomes almost impossible for a poet to exclude all sexual aura from this figure. Thus, readers can be shocked by the closing of a rose in Sylvia Plath's "Edge" without being at all surprised by her choice of metaphor. As I mentioned earlier, the poem describes or envisions the ancient statue of a dead woman with whom the speaker identifies. She has two children:

6. Ernst Kris, *Psychoanalytic Explorations in Art* (Bloomington: University of Indiana Press, 1962), p. 244.

> Each dead child coiled, a white serpent,
> One at each little
>
> Pitcher of milk, now empty,
> She has folded
>
> Them back into her body as petals
> Of a rose close when the garden
>
> Stiffens and odours bleed
> From the sweet, deep throats of the night flower.

Soon to commit suicide, Sylvia Plath experiences a projective identification with her own children, returning them—and herself—to the place from which they came. A similar stability of reference to the body combines with a much greater range of abstraction in Blake's "The Sick Rose" to dramatize the global ravages of a repressed and corrupted sexuality.

> O Rose, thou art sick!
> The invisible worm
> That flies in the night
> In the howling storm,
>
> Has found out thy bed
> Of crimson joy:
> And his dark secret love
> Does thy life destroy.

Blake fuses, in one rose, the Body Sexual and the Body Politic and the Body Social and the Body Spiritual.

These pluckings must cease. They come to an end with the closing of another rose in a passage written by a poet who seldom failed to feel his thought as immediately as the odor of a rose. Shakespeare's lines are chaste ones. Othello speaks them to the "chaste stars" before he smothers Desdemona:

>   When I have plucked the rose,
> I cannot give it vital growth again,
> It needs must wither. I'll smell it on the tree. [kissing her]
> Ah, balmy breath that dost almost persuade
> Justice to break her sword! One more, one more!
> Be thus when thou art dead, and I will kill thee,
> And love thee after. One more, and that's the last.
> So sweet was ne'er so fatal.

These lines reveal how much Othello's love blends physical with spiritual passion, and hate with love. The lines reveal what must always be the case: how inevitably the physical and spiritual come together in the knotty stuff intrinsicate that is the language of poetry.

One word more, in the interests of accuracy. If on occasion in this chapter and elsewhere I use the phrase "sexual symbolism," let me in closing stress how misleading reifying such phraseology can be. Not only would it be illegitimate to speak of thorns and roses as "Freudian symbols," a common misnomer for "sexual symbols," one may even distort reality a bit by speaking of "sexual symbolism" for the very good reason that the phrase merely designates a *class* of symbols having a rather vague range of potential meaning.[7] Nouns used to designate concrete entities, like "thorn" and "rose," do not mislead, but nouns used to designate classes of things in the abstract, such as The Text as a class of hypothetical texts, or Freedom, as a class of specific liberties, can cause obfuscation unless great care is exercised. One man's text may turn out to be another's inkblot, one man's freedom another's tyranny. There would be less chance of confusion if one were to employ a verb in place of a noun by saying the poet *symbolizes* sexuality through certain imagery instead of saying he uses *sexual symbols.* What is at issue is not the existence of some highly reified, codified lexicon of prefabricated sexual symbols. What is at issue is the capacity of poets to encode their thoughts and feelings in any images they choose so long as they encode them with the immediacy of the odor of a rose in a way that the images may be decoded, or recreated, with equal immediacy by the reader of these traces—a reader who tracks the heart's own spoor.

7. In making this distinction I have in mind the article by Charles Rycroft entitled "Is Freudian Symbolism a Myth?" *New York Review of Books,* January 24, 1974, as well as Roy Schafer's emphasis on the dangers of reification in *A New Language for Psychoanalysis* (New Haven: Yale University Press, 1976).

EPILOGUE

The Poet's Tongue
of Flame

໒໐໐໐໐໐໐໐໐໐໐໐໐໐໐໐໐໐໐໐໐໐໐

O HEART! the aequall poise of love's both parts
Bigge alike with wounds and darts
Live in these conquering leaves; live all the same
And walk through all tongues one triumphant FLAME.
　　　　　　　—Crashaw, "The Flaming Heart"

Inspired by the Holy Ghost, the disciples achieve supernatural communication by speaking in tongues. As Hawthorne interprets this event, they speak not with the power of speech in foreign tongues but with a mysterious ability to address "the whole human brotherhood in the heart's native language." Hawthorne links Dimmesdale's comparable ability to reach the whole human brotherhood through the heart's native language with his artistic talent for speaking in the humble medium of familiar images. It would appear that inspiration is not enough. What distinguishes possessors of the Tongue of Flame is the inspired use they make of transferential imagery—of metaphor. Many themes associated in myth and literature with the component tropes of this master metaphor reflect the deeper, more obscure, more powerful currents of the transferential process. These themes come to mind.

　　Glossolalia, or babbling. The profoundest voices may be un-

131

clear. In the oracles of John Barth, "Ill fortune, constraint and terror, generate guileful art; despair inspires. The laureled clairvoyants tell our doom in riddles. Sewn in our robes are horrid tales, and the speakers-in-tongues enounce atrocious tidings. The prophet-birds seem to speak sagely, but are shrieking their frustration. The senselessest babble, could we ken it, might disclose a dark message, or prayer."[1]

Articulation. Poets articulate. Hawthorne tells us in "Rappaccini's Daughter" how Giovanni and Beatrice "had spoken love in those gushes of passion when their spirits darted forth in articulated breath like tongues of long-hidden flame." In articulated breath. "Articulation," a joining together, derives from the Latin word for a joint of the body. The spirits of Giovanni and Beatrice dart forth in articulated breath like tongues of flame. There are many paratactic jointings here: of tongues with flame, of spirit with flame, of passion with tongues of flame, of darting-forth with tongues of flame, of breath with tongues of flame, of verbal articulation with tongues of flame. At the root of the body image of the lovers' articulate tongues of flame lie some passionate connections between the nimble-jointedness of the lovers' tongues and the connectedness of their language.

Isomorphy. Poets locate resemblances of forms. One thing can be shaped like another: a flame can be tongue-like, a tongue flame-like. In the presence of difference, similarity of form generates ambiguity, and ambiguity, in this passage from *Two Gentlemen of Verona*, allows a tongue to be extended in meaning:

> That man that hath a tongue, I say, is no man
> If with his tongue he cannot win a woman.

In *Love's Labour's Lost*,

> Love's feeling is more soft and sensible
> Than are the tender horns of cockled snails.
> Love's tongue proves dainty Bacchus gross in taste.

Humpback Richard draws a parallel between verbal and bodily integrity when he declares in 3 *Henry VI*, "I am resolved / That Clifford's manhood lies upon his tongue." In the primary process, isomorphy constitutes a basis for articulation, for shapeful jointings.

1. John Barth, *Lost in the Funhouse* (Garden City: Doubleday, 1968), p. 115.

Desire. Not all resemblances are isomorphic ones. More common than the sexual tongue in literature is the more diffuse symbol of fire as desire. What thing is love? asks George Peele.

> What thing is love? for sure love is a thing.
> It is a prick, it is a sting.
> It is a pretty, pretty thing.
> It is a fire, it is a coal,
> Whose flame creeps in at every hole.

The fire of desire engulfs the lover in Marvell's "Damon the Mower," where the swain burns on the pyre of "Juliana's scorching beams":

> Oh what unusual Heats are here,
> Which thus our Sun-burn'd Meadows sear!
> The Grass-hopper its pipe gives ore;
> And hamstring'd Frogs can dance no more.
> But in the brook the green Frog wades;
> And Grass-hoppers seek out the shades.
> Only the snake, that kept within,
> Now glitters in its second skin.

Damon asks where he can pass the fires "Of the hot day, or hot desires" and wonders into what "cool Cave" he can descend. He finds moisture only in his own tears, and coolness only in "her Icy Breast."

Crashaw loves to play with fire, as in the St. Teresa poems. In the ornate firebird erotics of "Epithalamium" he speaks of the Phoenix maiden's frozen fruit "of faire desire / which flourisheth in mutuall fire, / 'gainst nature," and he treats us to mock mourning of "a matchlesse maydenhead / that now is dead":

> Yet Love in death did wayte upon her,
>   granting leave she should expire
> in her fumes, and have the honour
>   t'exhale in flames of his owne fire;
>   her funeral pyle
>   the marriage bedd,
>   in a sighed smile
>   she vanished.
> So rich a dress of death nere famed
> the Cradles where her kindred flamed;
> so sweet her mother phaenixes of th' East
>   nere spiced their neast.

In the prayerbook ode Crashaw tells of how the "subtil lightning"
of "soul-piercing glances" flies

> Home to the heart, and setts the house on fire
> And melts it down in sweet desire.

With the same rhyme Crashaw adapts conventional iconography
to his religious needs in another poem:

> Lord, when the sense of thy sweet grace
> Sends up my soul to seek thy face.
> Thy blessed eyes breed such desire.
> I dy in love's delicious Fire.

Fire as desire. In dreams, as compared to poetry, Everyman and
Everywoman possess the tongue of flame, as in this dream about
hot tongue: "A patient with a sore tongue dreamed of wanting a
piece of cold ham or hot tongue. The hot tongue meant the
tongue lashing she wanted to give her husband and analyst. It
meant the tongue as a substitute for the genital intercourse of
which her husband's impotence deprived her. It meant her old
dependent infantile relationship to her mother. It meant the
threat of punishment and death through the fantasy of a cancer of
the tongue. Here it meant an identification with Freud, in a
megalomaniac fulfillment of dreams of omniscience and omnipotence."[2]

Desire emerges as fire in the shared dreams called mythology.
One of the Australian myths recounted by Róheim in *The Gates
of the Dream* reads in part: "Larkaka (sheet lightning) went to
his aunt who lived at Tjakala. His aunt was an *alknarintja*. When
she saw Larkaka approach she danced shaking her thighs, causing
the lips of her vagina to tremble. Lightning came out of her
vagina. Larkaka entered her vagina. When Nkanjia spoke (thun-
dered) his penis became erect and fire came out of his penis
setting trees alight."[3] The word for sperm in one Australian tribe
is *wondjir*. Wondjina is a god of rain and fertility. "The Wondjina
Kalaru threw the first flash of lightning by splitting his penis and

2. Lawrence S. Kubie, quoted by Ludwig Von Bertalanffy, "On the Definition
of the Symbol," in *Psychology and the Symbol*, ed. Joseph R. Royce (New York:
Random House, 1965), p. 49.

3. Géza Róheim, *The Gates of the Dream* (New York: International Universities Press, 1969), pp. 104 and 110.

letting out the fire and the flash of lightning. He created the fire
by turning outside the red inside of the split penis and letting out
the fire and a flash of lightning."

Ire. Fire as ire. Fire can be hostile, consuming, devouring,
destructive, as in Sylvia Plath's "Lady Lazarus":

> I am your opus,
> I am your valuable,
> The pure gold baby
>
> That melts to a shriek.
> I turn and burn.
> Do not think I underestimate your great concern.
>
> Ash, ash—
> You poke and stir.
> Flesh, bone, there is nothing there—
>
> A cake of soap,
> A wedding ring,
> A gold filling.
>
> Herr God, Herr Lucifer,
> Beware.
> Beware.
>
> Out of the ash
> I rise with my red hair
> And I eat men like air.

In "Fever 103°" Sylvia Plath asks,

> Does not my heat astound you. And my light.
> All by myself I am a huge camellia
> Glowing and coming and going, flush on flush.
>
> I think I am going up,
> I think I may rise—
> The beads of hot metal fly, and I, love, I
>
> Am a pure acetylene
> Virgin
> Attended by roses,
>
> By kisses, by cherubim
> By whatever these pink things mean.

Worship. Fire worship. While tongues of flame can be aggressive and destructive, the themes of desire and worship appear
more often, as in the homey sketch of Hawthorne entitled "Fire

Worship." Hawthorne writes in praise of Fire: "It was so sweet of him, being endowed with such power, to dwell day after day, and one long lonesome night after another, on the dusky hearth, and only now and then betray his wild nature by thrusting his red tongue out of the chimney-top!"

There are many gods of fire. Among them is the one God of the ancient Hebrews. According to no less a Kabbalist than Harold Bloom, fire is one of the three major biblical tropes for God, the others being the voice and the chariot.[4]

Fire worshippers guard the sacral fire. "The sacral fire must be a virgin fire. Once a year, in the temple of Vesta, in observance of the feast of the virginal goddess who was the guardian of the hearth, the home, and the family, the sacral was kindled anew. It is obvious that the making of fire, not the fire as such, was the significant action of the ritual."[5]

Fire worship appears in an amusing folktale called "Jack and the Old Fire Dragon."[6] Unlike his fearful brothers, the hero, Jack, not only confronts the fireball-spitting dragon, he treats him with respect, calls him "Dad," and invites him to share dinner. Symbolizing Jack's acquisition of paternal fire-power in the second portion of the story is his victory over the old fire dragon with the aid of magic ointment that wards off fireballs and a magic silver sword, with which he beheads the dragon. Afterwards Jack and his brothers marry the three beautiful maidens who lived with the dragon.

"Jack and the Old Fire Dragon" constitutes a comic version of the Prometheus and Oedipus myths combined. A great mound of scholarship deals with myths about fire, including work by Gaston Bachelard, Ernest Jones, Norman O. Brown, and Sir James Frazer—Frazer devoting an entire book to the single subject of myths about the origin of fire.[7] One feature of these myths is that

4. Harold Bloom, *Poetry and Repression* (New Haven: Yale University Press, 1976), p. 87.

5. Theodore Thass-Thienemann, *Interpretation of Language* (New York: Jason Aronson, 1973) I, p. 313.

6. *Ray Hicks Telling Four Traditional "Jack Tales,"* Folk-Legacy Records, 1963.

7. Gaston Bachelard, *The Psychoanalysis of Fire*, trans. Alan C. M. Ross (Boston: Beacon Press, 1964); Ernest Jones, *Essays in Applied Psycho-Analysis* (New York: International Universities Press, 1964) II, pp. 306-14; Norman O.

the acquisition of fire by culture heroes is always a crime. In that respect the story of Prometheus is typical.

Procreation. While discussing Prometheus in "The Acquisition and Control of Fire," Freud retells the story of Servius Tullius. The legend deals with the parentage of the Roman king. Ocrisia, his mother, is a household slave of King Tarquin. When she makes an offering of cakes and libations on the royal hearth one day, so the story goes, a flame "in the shape of a male member shot out from the fire. . . . Ocrisia conceived by the god or spirit of the fire and in due time brought forth Servius Tullius." Hence flame fecundates. Besides the libidinal value Freud emphasizes in retelling the story, the flame has procreative significance.

Procreative fire. In mythology, the generative aspects of the fire of life fuse inseparably with the libidinal aspects. Karl Abraham marshals many details about the creative and procreative implications of fire symbolism in *Dreams and Myths*.[8] Fire is associated with the sun and with lightning. It descends from heaven. The movement of lightning suggests the flight of a bird, so fire becomes linked with various birds, especially the eagle, the hawk, and the woodpecker. The association of fire with body-warmth pervades mythology. Related to this idea is the fact that all Indo-Germanic peoples produced fire by rubbing or twirling a stick in the hollow of another piece of wood, a technological fact of life leading to the association of fire-making with procreative friction. The two parts of the primitive fire-making apparatus often bear the names of the male and female genitalia.

Gods in charge of fire appear at a later stage of cosmogony. In the Vedas the god Agni incorporates fire, light, the sun, and lightning. He is also the first man. In some versions he is the lightningbird. Picus, the woodpecker, is the firebird, lightning, and man in the oldest Latin myths, and later the god of lying-in women and sucklings. Matarichvan, whose name means "he who swells or works in the mother," can bring forth Agni when he is hidden in the clouds or the woods or in a cavern. Abraham says,

Brown, *Love's Body* (New York: Random House, 1966), pp. 176-83; Sir James George Frazer, *Myths of the Origin of Fire* (London: Macmillan, 1930).

8. Karl Abraham, *Dreams and Myths*, trans. William A. White (New York: Journal of Nervous and Mental Diseases Pub. Co., 1913), p. 21. I am also drawing on a paper of my own: "Prometheus as a Scapegoat," *Literature and Psychology* XI (Winter, 1961): 6-11.

Matarichvan, the fire-bringer, corresponds in the Greek myth to Prometheus. In historical times the name Prometheus, which has experienced various changes, has been interpreted as "fore-thought." As an older form he is, among other things, referred to as "Pramantha." This name has a double meaning. It signifies first the "forth-rubber," that is, one who through rubbing brings something forth.

Through rubbing he brings the fire forth and generates man. Here it is to be noted that "mantha" signifies the male genitals. The second meaning of Pramantha is the "fire-robber." Close to the idea that Prometheus-Pramantha created fire, is the other idea, that he—like Matarichvan—brought or stole the fire from heaven. He concealed the sparks in a shrub, that is, one of the sorts of wood that served for the creation of fire.

In the myth we thus see fire represented in three different forms: as fire (fire-god), as fire-maker (or rubber, or fetcher) and finally as man. [p. 31]

The Sanskrit word *pramantha* means the swastika, or fire-drill, which Prometheus is supposed to have invented.[9] Abraham concludes that fire appears in four forms in the saga: as heavenly fire, as earthly fire, as the fire of life, and as sexual fire.

Masculine and feminine forms of procreative fire appear in myth and folklore. "The household fire on the fireplace, however realistic this concept might be, is a feminine concept, while the imaginary inside fire, the sacral-religious 'Fire,' the god of fire, is definitely masculine," says Theodore Thass-Thienemann.[10] "The masculine inside fire is loaded with genital generative fantasies. These fantasies may also refer to the hearth or fireplace. For instance, in Old Slavic language the 'husband' is called *ogni-scaninu*, which properly means 'owner of the fireplace.' According to these fantasies, the fire is 'generated' or *kindled*. This verb *to kindle* means 'to set fire,' 'to inflame with passion,' 'to make ardent,' on the one hand, and 'to generate offspring' on the other hand. The latter is now said mainly of the brood of animals, but the corresponding German *Kind*, 'child,' refers to the human." According to Thass-Thienemann, our dictionaries attempt to separate these two kinds of kindlings, "but the meanings were not so neatly separated in the minds of the speakers as in dictionaries."

9. Robert Graves, *Greek Myths* (Baltimore: Penguin, 1955) I, p. 148.
10. Theodore Thass-Thienemann, *Interpretation of Language* I, pp. 312-13.

Inspiration. Artistic inspiration has always been associated with fire. M. H. Abrams says poetic inspiration differs from normal ideation in these ways: the process of composition is felt to be sudden and effortless; involuntary and automatic; accompanied by intense excitement, elation, or even rapture; and completed work seems somehow unfamiliar, as though written by someone else. "The earliest and most tenacious theory adduced to explain these phenomena attributed the poem to the dictation of a supernatural visitant."[11] Among the instances of such alleged visitation, says Abrams, "The Hebrew singers claimed that they kindled to communicate the word of God: 'I kept silent, yea even from good words. . . . And while I was thus musing, the fire kindled and at last I spoke with my tongue.'"

Inspiration promotes sublimation. The excitation accompanying the inspirational phase of artistic activity can be thought of as a transformation of the psychosexual forces being sublimated. The sense of one's own work being alien, as though produced by a visitation of the Muse, reflects the unconscious dynamics of the artistic process, the idea of an influencing Muse being a projection of this endopsychic activity. An influential Muse may also be thought of as the projection of an introjected mother—an indwelling principle of fertility, magically contained.

As Shakespeare tells us, lovers, lunatics, and poets have always been inspired, whether from without or within, and the best kind of communication is inspired communication, an idea implicit in the notion of a fostering Muse and explicit in Hawthorne's treatment of Dimmesdale's special gift of addressing the whole human brotherhood in the heart's native language. Inspired by guilt and residual passion, Dimmesdale communicates his secret sin through the humblest medium of familiar words and images.

Eloquence. Passion confers eloquence. Satan himself must therefore have spoken with passion, or out of passion, as he addressed himself to Eve. As he refers to the story, Norman O. Brown jokes about the tongue being the first unruly member: "Speech resexualized: overcoming the consequences of the fall. The tongue was the first unruly member. Displacement is first from above downwards; the penis is a symbolic tongue, and

11. M. H. Abrams, *The Mirror and the Lamp* (New York: Norton, 1958), p. 189.

disturbances of ejaculation a kind of genital stuttering. 'In the beginning the serpent, getting possession of the ears of Eve, thence spread his poison through her whole body; today Mary through her ears received the champion of everlasting bliss.' "[12]

Satan was eloquent. He was an articulate, nimble-jointed serpent. Similar associations of eloquence with sexual power probably underlie a magical ritual designed to convey the gift of eloquence. The superstition in question has it that the tongue of a male snake, cut from the serpent on St. George's Eve, confers the gift of eloquence on any person under whose tongue the serpent's tongue is placed.[13]

Róheim says he often encounters the phrase "the penis talks" in the texts of myths.[14]

Origins. Despite all the associations of linguistic and imaginative vitality with sexual force, it would be the grossest of phallic fallacies to forget that in the process of learning to speak, everyone's first motive for using language is to communicate with a nurturing, protecting Other. We all experience what Selma Fraiberg calls "the magic years," those early years when giant genie Others respond to our commands. Hence everyone possesses a magical tongue of flame almost from birth except for those unfortunate emotional outcasts who become autistic and who often relapse into mutism. Though much of the omnipotence of language wears off for most of us, traces of language's magic potentialities remain for man to re-experience through the words of those privileged few, the poets, who redevelop this linguistic omnipotence until it becomes a tongue of flame, a miraculous instrument for communication.

12. Norman O. Brown, *Love's Body*, p. 251.
13. Ernest Jones, *Essays in Applied Psycho-Analysis* II, p. 314.
14. Géza Róheim, *The Gates of the Dream*, p. 104.

Index

141